P9-DEC-243

The Readers' Advisory Guide
to Mystery

NEVADA COUNTY LIBRARY-GRASS VALLEY
DEC   2012

ALA READERS' ADVISORY SERIES

The Readers' Advisory Guide to Mystery, Second Edition

John Charles, Candace Clark,
Joanne Hamilton-Selway,
and Joanna Morrison

Joyce Saricks and Neal Wyatt
SERIES EDITORS

American Library Association
Chicago   2012

NEVADA COUNTY LIBRARY – GRASS VALLEY

© 2012 by the American Library Association. Any claim of copyright is subject to applicable limitations and exceptions, such as rights of fair use and library copying pursuant to Sections 107 and 108 of the U.S. Copyright Act. No copyright is claimed for content in the public domain, such as works of the U.S. government.

Printed in the United States of America

16 15 14 13 12   5 4 3 2 1

Extensive effort has gone into ensuring the reliability of the information in this book; however, the publisher makes no warranty, express or implied, with respect to the material contained herein.

ISBNs: 978-0-8389-1113-6 (paper); 978-0-8389-9390-3 (PDF); 978-0-8389-9391-0 (ePUB); 978-0-8389-9392-7 (Mobipocket); 978-0-8389-9393-4 (Kindle). For more information on digital formats, visit the ALA Store at alastore.ala.org and select eEditions.

Library of Congress Cataloging-in-Publication Data
Charles, John, 1962–
    [Mystery readers' advisory]
    The readers' advisory guide to mystery / John Charles, Candace Clark, Joanne Hamilton-Selway, and Joanna Morrison. — Second edition.
        pages   cm. — (ALA Editions' readers' advisory series)
    Revision of: The mystery readers' advisory : the librarian's clues to murder and mayhem / John Charles, Joanna Morrison, [and] Candace Clark. — Chicago : American Library Association, 2002.
    Includes bibliographical references and index.
    ISBN 978-0-8389-1113-6
    1. Fiction in libraries—United States. 2. Libraries—United States—Special collections—Detective and mystery stories. 3. Readers' advisory services—United States. 4. Detective and mystery stories—Bibliography. I. Clark, Candace, 1950– II. Hamilton-Selway, Joanne. III. Morrison, Joanna. IV. Title.
    Z711.5.C48 2012
    025.2'78088372—dc23   2011042501

Cover image © Andrea Danti/Shutterstock, Inc.

♾ This paper meets the requirements of ANSI/NISO Z39.48-1992 (Permanence of Paper).

ALA Editions purchases fund advocacy, awareness, and accreditation programs for library professionals worldwide.

CONTENTS

SERIES INTRODUCTION

Joyce Saricks and Neal Wyatt, Series Editors

In a library world in which finding answers to readers' advisory questions is often considered among our most daunting service challenges, library staff need guides that are supportive, accessible, and immediately useful. The titles in this series are designed to be just that. They help advisors become familiar with fiction genres and nonfiction subjects, especially those they don't personally read. They provide ready-made lists of "need-to-know" elements such as key authors and read-alikes, as well as tips on how to keep up with trends and important new authors and titles.

Written by librarians with years of RA experience who are also enthusiasts of the genre or subject, the titles in this series of practical guides emphasize an appreciation of the topic, focusing on the elements and features fans enjoy so advisors unfamiliar with the topics can readily appreciate why they are so popular.

Because this series values the fundamental concepts of readers' advisory work and its potential to serve readers, viewers, and listeners in whatever future space libraries inhabit, the focus of each book is on appeal and how appeal crosses genre, subject, and format, especially to include audio and video, as well as graphic novels. Thus, each guide emphasizes the importance of whole-collection readers' advisory and explores ways to make suggestions that include novels, nonfiction, and multimedia, as well as ways to incorporate whole-collection elements into displays and booklists.

Each guide includes sections designed to help librarians in their RA duties, be that daily work or occasional interactions. Topics covered in each volume include the following:

- The appeal of the genre or subject and information on subgenres and types so that librarians might understand the breadth and scope of the topic and how it relates to other genres and subjects. Each volume also includes a brief history to give advisors context and highlight beloved classic titles.

- Descriptions of key authors and titles with explanations of why they're important, why advisors should be familiar with them, and why they should be kept in our collections. Lists of read-alikes accompany these core author and title lists, which allows advisors to move from identifying a key author to helping patrons find new authors to enjoy.

- Information on how to conduct the RA conversation so that advisors can learn the tools and skills needed to develop deeper connections between their collections and their communities of readers, listeners, and viewers.

- A crash course in the genre or subject designed to get staff up to speed. Turn to this section to get a quick overview of the genre or subject, as well as a list of key authors and read-alikes.

- Resources and techniques for keeping up to date and understanding new developments in the genre or subject are also provided. These will not only aid staff already familiar with the genre or subject but also help those not familiar learn how to become so.

- Tips for marketing collections and lists of resources and awards round out the tools staff need to be successful working with their community.

■ ■ ■ ■ ■

As readers who just happen to be readers' advisors, we hope that the guides in this series lead to longer to-be-read, watched, and listened-to lists. Our goal is that the series helps those new to RA feel supported and less at sea and introduces new ideas, or new ways of looking at foundational concepts, to advisors who have been at this for a while. Most of all, we hope that this series helps advisors feel excited and eager to help patrons find their next great title. So dig in, explore, and learn and enjoy the almost-alchemical process of connecting title and reader.

PREFACE

It doesn't take Sherlock Holmes to deduce that mysteries are popular with readers. Whether it is the wealth of mystery authors who regularly appear on best-seller lists, or even just the number of readers in your own library who ask, "Where are the mysteries?" it is clear that this genre is hot.

The purpose of this book is simple: to provide an introduction to the mystery genre and to offer some basic tips on providing effective mystery readers' advisory service. This book is not intended to be a comprehensive bibliography of the mystery genre; there are many excellent titles suited to that task (several of which we include in our resources section). In our book, we offer a selection of key authors and titles in the genre, those constituting a core collection and a baseline for understanding the genre, but this focus is only a sampling, a tantalizing taste, if you will, of the literary banquet that awaits the mystery fan.

Mysteries and the adrenaline-rush genres of suspense and thrillers are closely connected in many ways. Some authors write in multiple genres, and many readers are dedicated fans of each kind of novel. Our book focuses solely on the mystery genre itself. We occasionally discuss the suspense or thriller novel in connection with mystery fiction, but a separate readers' advisory book on adrenaline novels is in the works as part of this series.

In the belief that understanding the roots of a genre can help place authors and titles in historical context, we have included a short history of the mystery. Our history is not a definitive chronology of the genre but rather an introduction that will help the novice mystery readers' advisor understand some of the key authors and literary elements of this genre.

One of the things that quickly became most apparent to us as we wrote this book is that defining the mystery, as well as deciding how to subdivide the genre, is difficult, exhausting work (at the very least our friends and coworkers soon grew exhausted listening to us complain about it). We quickly found that one person's cozy mystery might be another person's traditional detective story. One readers' advisory source might catalog mysteries by theme, whereas another might use type of detective to subdivide the genre. Our definitions of the mystery genre are just that—ours.

If another definition or subdivision works better for you and your readers, we encourage you to use that instead. Readers' advisory work is part art and part science, and you should always be flexible when it comes to adapting readers' advisory tools and materials to your own working environment.

A FEW WORDS ABOUT THE FORMAT OF THIS BOOK

As noted already, this book is not intended to be an exhaustive study of the mystery genre but instead is a guide that will help library staff new to mystery fiction get started working with readers. After chapters devoted to the history of the genre and its appeal, there are chapters dedicated to the four different subgenres (as we classify them) of mysteries: amateur sleuths, private investigators, procedural detectives, and historical sleuths.

One of the most intimidating things about mystery readers' advisory work—especially if you are new to the genre—is the seemingly overwhelming number of authors and titles that readers expect you to know. In each of the subgenre chapters, we include a section called "Key Authors." The intent of this section is to provide information on some of the most popular mystery authors writing within each subgenre. For each key author we also offer a "Now Read" author with the intention that if readers have read everything by a particular key author, they might enjoy this author as well. The key authors and now-read authors we have chosen to include are just a sampling of the literary diversity and richness of the mystery genre. Our intentions are not to state that these authors are the only ones with whom readers' advisory staff should be familiar, but rather this is our way of introducing some of the more important authors in the mystery genre to you.

In addition to chapters on the mystery readers' advisory interview, collection development, and merchandising of your mystery collection, we have included a chapter dedicated to different resources—both print and web based—that can be useful when working with readers. We have also included a select bibliography at the end, which contains not only the print resources in the "Mystery Resources" chapter but also all of the references we consulted while writing this book. And for anyone faced with a time crunch, we have written a crash course in mystery fiction that provides enough basic information about the genre to get you started working with readers.

Readers' advisory work is filled with potential literary perils as well as plenty of opportunity for professional pratfalls (and we do admit in our many, many years working in libraries, we have hit most of those pratfalls!), but there is no denying the satisfaction that comes from having readers come back and tell us how much they enjoyed a book we suggested. So as we begin our possibly perilous journey into the world of mystery and crime, let us hearken to these inspiring words from that immortal detective Sherlock Holmes: "Come, Watson, come. The game is afoot!"

ACKNOWLEDGMENTS

We thank the following people for their invaluable contributions to this book:

Joyce Saricks and Neal Wyatt—two terrifically talented editors who pushed us into making this a better book.

Katherine Faydash—for her invaluable assistance and expert copy editing.

Shelley Mosley—an outstanding writer and a true friend (everyone needs a "comma queen" in their life).

Dorothy Pulkrabek and Carolyn Butler—valued friends who have the gift for knowing when to speak and when to listen.

The staff at the Scottsdale Public Library, who have supported this project—especially Katie O'Connor and Rebekka Jones, for her helpful assistance with the mystery television section and her thoughts on genre-blended mysteries.

The staff at the Poisoned Pen Mystery Bookstore—for all their always-helpful suggestions and their always-superb service.

1

DETECTING THE ENDURING APPEAL
OF THE MYSTERY NOVEL

At its simplest level, a mystery is any book in which some type of crime has been committed and someone attempts to solve the foresaid mystery, that is, discover who, how, and or why the crime was committed. Of course, in the mystery genre, there are endless variations of this basic formula.

Some people believe that all mysteries must include a murder, but this is not always so. Although murder is the most frequently found crime in mystery novels, there are any number of books that craft excellent mysteries around crimes other than homicide. For example, in Josephine Tey's *The Franchise Affair*, it is a reputation that is killed rather than a person. *Aunt Dimity's Death*, by Nancy Atherton, is one of our favorite mysteries of all time, but there is no murder in this modern cozy classic. Donald Westlake has written several excellent caper novels, including *The Hot Rock*, which contain not one dead body. Dorothy L. Sayers's *The Gaudy Night* features her celebrated detecting duo of Lord Peter Wimsey and Harriet Vane, but the book focuses on vandalism at a women's college in Oxford instead of Sayers's usual plot, which centers on murder most foul. And in Earlene Fowler's *Mariner's Compass* there are mysteries aplenty but no murders.

Although many of your patrons read both mystery and suspense novels (and some authors write both types of fiction), there is a distinct difference between the fiction genres. The easiest way to understand the difference between mysteries and suspense novels is to think about the timeline of the book. In a mystery novel, the focus of the story is on solving the crime. In a suspense novel, the focus is on preventing a crime from happening or escaping from the criminal. In a mystery, the protagonist tries to figure out who the murderer is, whereas in most all suspense novels, the protagonist (or at least the reader) all too often knows who the real murderer is, and the plot centers on how the protagonist escapes from becoming the killer's next victim.

Thrillers are just suspense novels taken to the next level. In a typical suspense novel, the object of the villain's wrath is an individual or a small group of people, whereas in a thriller, the literary stakes are higher, as a whole city, country, or even the world is in danger. As you work with mystery readers, you will frequently find yourself crossing over into suspense and thriller country, but for this book, we limit our discussion to just the mystery genre.

In the past two decades, there has been another literary shift in the mystery genre as more and more mystery authors begin to call their books crime fiction. Although crime fiction has been a part of the mystery genre for more than half a century, there are some differences between these two kinds of books. In a crime novel, the focus shifts from a strict attempt to solve the puzzle to an exploration of the psychology motivating the individuals involved in the story. James M. Cain is famous for his noirish tales of greed and deception, including the classics *The Postman Always Rings Twice* and *Double Indemnity*. Elmore Leonard built his literary reputation creating novels about criminals trying to score, including *Killshot* and *Rum Punch*. With more of an emphasis on characterization and less concern about the restoration of social order found in traditional mysteries, crime fiction can push the mystery genre closer to the world of literary fiction, but readers who expect a traditional mystery might not always be thrilled with this brand of crime novels.

WHY READERS ARE DRAWN TO MYSTERIES: AN APPEAL PERSPECTIVE

Mysteries offer the reader a world in which justice and order prevail. They are, in many ways, a modern version of the medieval morality play, in which good and evil battle for dominance. All too often in the real world, justice is not served and order is not restored. How very satisfying, then, for many readers to see the reverse come true in mystery fiction. This orderly structure of the mystery genre is a powerful element of a book's appeal for many readers.

For some mystery readers, it is all about the puzzle. These readers want a plot that challenges them to solve the crime, using clues the author has woven into the story, before the author's fictional detective finds out who dunit. Puzzle-based mysteries have had a major role in the genre almost since the beginning, and some of the genre's most influential writers have been expert puzzle crafters, including Agatha Christie and Ellery Queen. This doesn't mean that these authors are less skilled at creating interesting characters and realistically detailed settings—it simply means that a clever plot is the key to the whole book. An excellent example of this is the works of the author G. M. Malliet. Her three mysteries featuring Detective Chief Inspector St. Just have an irresistible mix of acerbic wit and engaging characters, but Malliet also delivers soundly constructed plots with plenty of red herrings that challenge readers to guess who dunit.

The pleasure of solving a puzzle-based mystery is certainly one reason readers are drawn to this genre, but it is not the only one. For other readers, intriguing characters are the most important part of the story. Whether it is Sue Grafton's iconic Kinsey Millhone, or Elizabeth Peters's Amelia Peabody, or Rita Mae Brown's sleuthing cat-and-dog combo of Mrs. Murphy and Tee Tucker, readers just want to spend time with these characters. Just think of how many readers could care less what actual mystery Janet Evanovich's Stephanie Plum may have gotten herself entangled in but deeply enjoy catching up with the zany antics of the New Jersey bounty hunter and her crazy cohorts.

The intrinsic appeal of the characters goes a long way in explaining the appeal of the mystery series, as it allows readers to get to know a sleuth through several volumes of work and watch the changes in their "life." For some mystery readers, these fictional detectives become as real to them as their neighbors or friends (some even go so far as to write letters to the characters). The attachment of readers to their favorite sleuth is nothing new. Perhaps the most celebrated example of this occurred when Sir Arthur Conan Doyle, tired of writing mysteries, tried to kill off his literary creation, Sherlock Holmes, at Reichenbach Falls at the end of *The Memoirs of Sherlock Holmes*. The public outcry was so great that Doyle was forced to bring Holmes back with the publication of *The Return of Sherlock Holmes*.

Setting or geographic locale is not always a primary factor when it comes to selecting a mystery, but it can be an important reason some readers choose a book. Certain mystery writers are known for their ability to vividly re-create a locale or setting, and their readers come to expect this vibrant setting as part of the story. The Appalachian Mountains backdrop of Sharyn McCrumb's Ballad series is as important to McCrumb's story as the characters or plot of each book. Margaret Maron has written two different mystery series, but her readers especially value her Deborah Knott books, not only for their wonderful characters but also for the expertly detailed North Carolina setting that infuses these books with their distinctive flavor. Tony Hillerman is an award-winning mystery novelist whose books combine superiorly crafted plots with a rich cast of characters. But what many readers remember most about his books is the New Mexico setting and its strong ties to the Navajo culture. And reading Cara Black's series featuring Aimée Léduc, each book of which focuses on a different section of Paris, is almost as good as taking a trip to France.

Mystery readers also like that fact that they often learn something while reading their favorite novels. Many mystery novelists use their own individual expertise in a particular subject area to give their books a unique flavor. Jonathan Gash is known for giving readers a crash course on antiques and collectibles in his books featuring antiques "dealer" Lovejoy. In each of their cleverly crafted books, the writing team of Emma Lathen uses a different area of business, such as the commodities market and agriculture, as the novel's backdrop, proving that economics and business are not just topics for the *Wall Street Journal*. In the past decade, a whole slew of craft mysteries have been published, such as Monica Ferris's Needlecraft Mysteries, which provide the reader with intriguing details about everything from knitting and stained-glass crafting to apple growing and home repair work.

Perhaps, though, more than anything, the reason mysteries are popular is that they are simply good reads. At a time when writing style often trumps characterization and plotting in literary fiction, mystery authors know the power of an entertaining story. And readers know they can count on mystery authors and their books to keep them turning the pages.

2

THE HISTORY OF MYSTERY

Determining exactly when mysteries became a distinct literary genre of their own can be something of a mystery itself. Some critics, including author Dorothy L. Sayers, point to evidence of mystery elements in certain stories of the Bible. Others, such as Julian Symons, credit William Godwin's *Caleb Williams*, published in 1794, as the first true detective novel. But for our money, we think Edgar Allan Poe (or Ed as his friends called him) deserves kudos as the founding father of the mystery genre.

Poe first introduced his fictional sleuth, C. Auguste Dupin, in his 1841 short story "The Murders in the Rue Morgue." Poe continued Dupin's exploits in detective work in other stories, including "The Mystery of Marie Roget," published in 1842, and "The Purloined Letter," in 1845. In these works, Poe created many of the classic plot components of the mystery genre, such as the locked-room mystery and the use of a brilliant, eccentric detective who solves crimes through the use of deductive reasoning and the careful examination of clues, key genre elements that mystery writers still use today.

Poe's works inspired other novelists of his day, including Charles Dickens and Wilkie Collins, but men were not the only ones scribbling away at detective stories. In America, Metta Victoria Fuller Victor, writing as Seeley Regester, is credited with creating the first American detective novel, *The Dead Letter*, which was serialized in magazines and then published in book format in 1867. Fellow American writer Anna Katherine Green followed with her own book in 1878, *The Leavenworth Case, a Lawyer's Story*, introducing the first case of a body in the library to mystery readers.

Perhaps the most celebrated mystery writer of the late nineteenth century, and an author whose classic tales are still read today, is Sir Arthur Conan Doyle. With the publication in 1887 of Doyle's *A Study in Scarlet*, readers were introduced to an irresistibly clever detective who put his own stamp on the genre. With his quirky mannerisms and unique flair for crime solving, Sherlock Holmes and his sleuthing sidekick, Dr. Watson, quickly became favorites of readers around the globe.

The 1920s ushered in the Golden Age of detective fiction and saw the debut of one the genre's most famous authors, Agatha Christie. Christie wrote her first novel, *The Mysterious Affair at Styles*, after being challenged by her sister Madge, who didn't believe Agatha could finish a book, let alone get it published. Debuting in 1920, the book introduced readers to the former Belgian police detective turned private eye Hercule Poirot. Christie would go on to create several more series characters, including quintessential spinster sleuth Miss Marple and partners in detection (and marriage) Tommy and Tuppence Beresford. Almost every one of Christie's books earned a place on best-seller lists on both sides of the Atlantic, and her detective stories came to represent the genre for millions of readers. Christie, along with fellow British mystery writers Dorothy L. Sayers, Margery Allingham, and Ngaio Marsh eventually became known as the Queens of Crime.

Across the Atlantic, American mystery writers such as S. S. Van Dine, Ellery Queen, and John Dickson Carr followed the pattern established by the British Queens of Crime and turned out dozens of traditional mysteries in which brainpower rather than brute strength becomes the necessary means of solving a crime. From the least likely suspect to the most likely, these authors created entertaining puzzle-based mysteries that kept readers hooked and continue to do so even today. These Golden Age authors also introduced to the genre a number of quirky detectives, whose unusual mannerisms or eccentric personalities gave their mystery stories their distinct flavor. One example of this type of sleuth is Earl Derr Biggers's sleuth, Charlie Chan, a Chinese American police detective based in Hawaii, whose frequent use of Confucian quotes such as "the fool in a hurry drinks his tea with the fork" helps him solve mysteries. Another example is Rex Stout's Nero Wolfe, who rarely leaves his New York City brownstone, his orchids, and his gourmet meals to solve a crime but instead almost always relies on his partner, Archie Goodwin, to do the legwork, across thirty-three novels and forty novellas.

At the same time these traditional detective novels of manners were gaining in popularity, another type of mystery fiction was entering the scene. The hard-boiled mystery was born in the 1920s with the rise of popular magazines known as pulps. *Black Mask*, the most famous of these pulp magazines, began by offering readers adventure stories, but it soon devoted most of its pages to detective stories. The magazine's contributors included Dashiell Hammett, Raymond Chandler, and Mickey Spillane, all of whom would go on to successful careers as mystery novelists. Their work became known as hard boiled because, in writing about their fictional private-eye detectives, these authors strove to reflect the gritty day-to-day realities of life in the 1930s. Their literary detectives were rough, tough guys who had their own code of honor and were the complete opposite of the civilized sleuths created by authors such as Ellery Queen and Dorothy L. Sayers.

The police procedural subgenre really came into being in the 1940s. Although some Golden Age mystery authors, such as Ngaio Marsh, used a policeman as a detective, their cop sleuths in many ways really worked the same way as their amateur counterparts, and for the most part, there were not a lot of police procedures in these mysteries. In the years after World War II, however, authors such as Lawrence Treat, Hilary Waugh, Dell Shannon, and Ed McBain took a different approach to the police officer as a sleuth. These authors' books brought readers into the real world of the police force, showing how these cops, both as individuals and as part of a team, solved crimes.

In the 1970s, just as in society itself, diversity and change came to the mystery genre. Private-eye novels once again were in vogue, as fictional gumshoes discovered their softer sides. Authors such as Robert B. Parker introduced a more modern (and introspective) variation of the classic hard-boiled detective with his Boston-based PI Spenser. With the publication of *Fadeout* in 1970, Joseph Hansen offered readers one of the first mysteries to portray a gay detective in a positive and honest manner.

During this decade, women also began to gain a foothold in the private-eye subgenre as well. The British mystery writer P. D. James wrote her first Cordelia Gray novel, *An Unsuitable Job for a Woman*, in 1972, but many credit Marcia Muller, who wrote her debut Sharon McCone mystery, *Edwin of the Iron Shoes*, in 1977, with introducing readers to a new breed of female private eye. With the publication of the first books in their own series in 1982, the authors Sue Grafton and Sara Paretsky helped cement the place female detectives had gained in the gritty world of private eyes.

The 1970s also saw the mystery genre gain new depths in terms of the settings it offered readers. An excellent example of this is Tony Hillerman, who took readers to the Navajo reservation with the publication of his book *The Blessing Way* in 1970. For many readers, this was their first experience with an American mystery that was not set in one of the genre's two traditional locales: New York or Los Angeles. The growing popularity of Hillerman's books demonstrated to publishers that readers were interested in other cultures and other geographic settings.

Going back in time to solve crimes also became popular during the 1970s. Peter Lovesey opened the decade with the publication of his book *Wobble to Death*, set in Victorian England and featuring Sergeant Cribb and his assistant, Constable Thackery. Ellis Peters's Brother Cadfael medieval mysteries also got their start in 1970, with *A Morbid Taste for Bones* (although it would take seven years for the book to make its way to America). Elizabeth Peters introduced her intrepid late-nineteenth-century sleuth, Amelia Peabody, in 1975 with *A Crocodile on the Sandbank*, and by the decade's close, Anne Perry had delivered her first mystery featuring the Victorian sleuthing couple Charlotte and Thomas Pitt, *A Cater Street Hangman*.

The 1980s built on all these developments as the mystery genre became even more popular with readers. One notable development was the return to fashion of the cozy mystery (i.e., a mystery written without any graphic violence, language, or sex). Even though they had been around for decades, the 1980s saw an increased demand for traditional, or "cozy," mystery novels. In 1982, Virginia Rich penned her first book, *The Cooking School Murders*, giving readers a taste of the culinary crime novel. Joan Hess wrote her first mystery, *Strangled Prose*, featuring the Arkansas bookseller Claire Malloy, and in the 1980s Carolyn G. Hart introduced readers to the bookstore owner and amateur sleuth Annie Laurence Darling in *Death on Demand*.

The 1990s proved the new Golden Age of mystery fiction as a genre. New authors such as Nevada Barr, Dana Stabenow, and Jan Burke published their first mysteries. The beginning of this decade also saw the arrival of Patricia Cornwell, whose first Kay Scarpetta novel, *Postmortem*, swept the mystery awards field, inspired a new interest in forensics, and introduced the concept of the author as celebrity. Cornwell's meteoric climb up the best-seller charts reflected the ability for mysteries of all kinds—from Lilian Jackson Braun's cozy cat series to John Sandford's gritty police procedurals—to achieve permanent places on the *New York Times* best-seller list.

As the 1990s gave way to a new century, change continued to be the theme of the mystery genre. Blurring between fiction genres introduced readers to the idea of nontraditional mystery sleuths, such as Jim Butcher's wizard private eye, Harry Dresden, and J. D. Robb's (in reality romance writer Nora Roberts's) twenty-first-century NYPD lieutenant Eve Dallas. And in the twenty-first century, there has been a fundamental shift in the genre itself as more readers have become intrigued with the idea of reading a crime story rather than just a mystery novel. As the mystery genre begins its third century, the only guarantee we can offer is that there will be many exciting new authors and books ahead.

3

A CRASH COURSE IN
MYSTERY READERS' ADVISORY WORK

In a mystery, some type of crime is committed, and then a detective, whether an amateur sleuth or some type of professional such as a private investigator or a police officer, tries to solve the crime. Many mysteries can also be thought of as a literary form of the jigsaw puzzle. The fictional detective is searching for different pieces, or clues, if you will, of the mystery puzzle. Once the detective has acquired these pieces, he or she attempts to put them together to figure out who did it, how it was done, and why.

As you begin working with mystery readers, you will quickly discover the incredible diversity of the mystery genre, which offers readers everything from classic, traditional mysteries in which the whole point is competing with the fictional detective in a literary race find out who dunit to today's crime novels that focus more on the who—characters and their motivation—and less on putting the pieces of a fictional puzzle together to solve the actual crime. Last, although most mysteries do center on a murder investigation, not every mystery must include a murder.

HOW DOES A MYSTERY DIFFER FROM SUSPENSE NOVELS AND THRILLERS?

The easiest way to understand the difference between mysteries and suspense novels is to think of the book's plot in terms of "before" and "after." In a mystery novel, the focus of the story is on solving the crime. Almost all of the action takes place after the crime has been committed. In a suspense novel, the focus is on preventing a crime from happening. The protagonist's whole raison d'être in a suspense novel or thriller is on stopping the antagonist before he or she completes a crime. In a mystery, the protagonist tries to figure out who the villain is, whereas in most all suspense novels, the protagonist (or at least the reader) all too often knows who the real villain is, and the plot centers on how the protagonist escapes from becoming the next victim. Thrillers are just suspense novels taken up a few levels in the scope of the plot. In a typical suspense novel, the object of the villain's wrath is an individual or a small group of people, whereas in a thriller, the stakes are higher, as a whole city, country, or even the world is in danger.

FIVE AUTHORS AND TITLES EVERYONE NEEDS TO KNOW

First of all, coming up with five mystery authors and titles everyone should know in any fiction genre is not an easy task, and we are certain that there will be some readers' advisors who disagree with our choices. But the whole point of our choices is that if you—or a coworker—know absolutely nothing about mystery fiction, these authors and titles will get you started working with mystery readers.

Our Top Five Mystery Authors

Agatha Christie

Agatha Christie is known as the Queen of Crime for a reason: no one—not even that literary slacker James Patterson—has sold more mysteries than Agatha Christie. She invented two of the genre's most famous sleuths— the retired Belgium police detective turned private eye Hercule Poirot and the spinster sleuth extraordinaire Miss Jane Marple—and she wrote some of the most devilishly puzzling plots in the genre. Although some might quibble that other Golden Age mystery writers, such as Dorothy L. Sayers or Ngaio Marsh, deserve equal footing with Christie, they are missing the boat, so to speak. What makes Christie's books unique is that, first and foremost, Christie never forgot the key reason her fans read mysteries. Everything in her books is connected—even though you might not think so at first—to the question of who dunit. Christie devised classic, traditional mysteries that continue to delight readers nearly a century after her first book, *The Mysterious Affair at Styles*, debuted in 1920.

Robert B. Parker

Parker's most famous fictional creation (and one of the mystery genre's most unforgettable detectives) is the Boston-based private investigator Spenser. No first name, just Spenser. Introduced in *The Godwulf Manuscript* in 1972, Spenser is cast from the mold of the private eyes of Raymond Chandler's world. He's a tough guy with a code of honor but a socially enlightened conscience. In addition to being a "modern" version of the classic private eye, Spenser differed from his literary counterparts in another way: he didn't work completely alone. Spenser had his own support team, in the form of Hawk, his right-hand man with a shady, dangerous past, and his psychologist girlfriend, Susan Silverman. In contrast to the love-'em-and-leave-'em attitude of most hard-boiled gumshoes, the romantic relationship between Spenser and Silverman is refreshingly mature—and modern; one that can be traced through the novels. In addition, Boston is more than Spenser's home (and Parker's own home, too); it is a colorful backdrop to Spenser's life and his investigations, and the author's spare, yet atmospheric writing style flows perfectly with the story lines. Parker has created other characters, including private eye Sunny Randall and police chief Jesse Stone, but Spenser is his lasting legacy to mystery fiction.

Sue Grafton

Kinsey Millhone, Sue Grafton's tough, smart, and smart-mouthed fictional creation, was not the first female private investigator to grace the literary stage when she appeared in *A Is for Alibi* in 1982 (and she certainly will not be the last), but more so than any other character, Kinsey has come to represent the female gumshoe for millions of readers. A former cop turned private eye, the twice-divorced Kinsey is every man's equal and no man's fool when it comes to solving crimes, but what many readers love most about Kinsey are the small details about her life—like her beat-up Volkswagen and her ongoing love of Quarter Pounders with Cheese—that make Kinsey seem just like their best friend. Grafton successfully lightens up the traditionally darker tone of the hard-boiled school of private detection with Kinsey's wry sense of humor, but Grafton doesn't downplay the very real effects that violence can have on anyone's life, including Kinsey's. Dashiell Hammett and Raymond Chandler might have created the literary blueprint for the classic private eye, but with her Kinsey Millhone books, Sue Grafton has proved that anything a man can do, a woman can do better.

Tony Hillerman

Hillerman's quietly powerful books featuring Sergeant Jim Chee and Lieutenant Joe Leaphorn deserve a place on the top-five list for several reasons. With his Chee and Leaphorn series, which has introduced millions of readers to the fascinating world of the Navajo people, Hillerman proved that mystery readers were willing to try a procedural that wasn't set in either New York City or Los Angeles. Hillerman's ability to bring the Southwestern landscape to life in his books also demonstrates how important a sense of place can be in a mystery. In many ways, Hillerman's mysteries are as much about the traditional and contemporary culture and customs of the Navajo and about how Chee's and Leaphorn's understanding of their world is vital to solving the crime. This discovery aspect of the books is another factor that many readers—some of whom have never picked up a mystery before—love: the chance to learn more about something, be it a place, a people, or a culture, while enjoying a great mystery.

Michael Connelly

There are plenty of writers staking out a place in the world of police procedurals today, but none of them has consistently hit a chord with readers as has Michael Connelly. There is a definite literary link in Connelly's books that feature Hieronymus "Harry" Bosch to other genre greats such as Raymond Chandler and Joseph Wambaugh (as well as a bit of James Ellroy, if you ask us), but Connelly's work is distinctively his own. Using his experiences working as a police reporter at the *Los Angeles Times*, Connelly gives his character-driven Bosch books a vivid sense of gritty realism as he writes about the day-to-day struggles all cops endure as they try to clear their never-ending caseload. Connelly takes the fascinating world of police detective work; adds a complicated, conflicted protagonist; sets it against the colorful world of Los Angeles; and creates mystery magic.

Five Mysteries Everyone Should Read

Murder at the Vicarage, by Agatha Christie

Yes, we know there are other titles, such as *The Murder of Roger Ackroyd*, *And Then There Were None*, and even *Murder on the Orient Express*, that equally deserve this space, but for our money, this is the one Christie to read if you never read anything else by her. *Murder at the Vicarage* introduced the spinster sleuth par excellence, the deliciously tart-tongued Miss Marple and her world of St. Mary Mead to mystery readers, and the genre has never been the same since. Christie is all about the cleverly placed clue, and *Murder at the Vicarage* shows her at the top of her literary game: it seems everyone in the village wanted to murder annoying Colonel Prothero, but everyone seems to have an unbreakable alibi. Leave it to Miss Marple to find the killer!

Devil in a Blue Dress, by Walter Mosley

It isn't easy to integrate social commentary into a compelling story, but Mosley consistently does so with his series featuring the African American sleuth Ezekiel "Easy" Rawlins. Set against the racially torn LA of the 1940s, '50s, and '60s, Easy finds himself reluctantly taking on a number of cases that are often solved more because of his own connections and knowledge of the African American community than because of his actual detective skills. From *Devil in a Blue Dress*, in which a rich white man hires Easy to find his mistress, to his latest case, Mosley writes character-rich detective stories that vividly and honestly narrate the day-to-day struggles many people face in America.

The No. 1 Ladies' Detective Agency, by Alexander McCall Smith

OK, we can immediately hear the cries as to why we would put this book on the top five and thus leave out so many other amazing mysteries. The reason is simple: with this novel Alexander McCall Smith introduced millions of readers, who might never have chosen a mystery on their own, to the genre. A brilliant combination of both cozy mystery and a warm and fuzzy gentle read, *The No. 1 Ladies' Detective Agency* gave the mystery genre the uniquely endearing heroine Mma Precious Ramotswe, who, with the help of her assistant Mma Makutsi and J. L. B Matekoni, begins what will hopefully be a long and successful career in detection. Mysteries are all about solving the crime and restoring order to the social system. Mma Ramotswe not only closes her cases; she restores order to the very lives of her clients.

Farewell, My Lovely, by Raymond Chandler

We all agree (OK, three of the four of us writing this book agree, which is something like four out of five dentists agreeing) that Dashiell Hammett "invented" the private-eye subgenre and that *The Maltese Falcon* is a classic mystery. But if you read only one PI novel, it has to be one of Chandler's books, like *Farewell, My Lovely,* in which private detective Philip Marlowe's latest case involves finding Moose Malloy's missing girlfriend, Velma. Chandler took everything Hammett brought to the world of mystery fiction and then added his own impossibly elegant writing style and ironic literary attitude to the mix, taking the detective novel into the realm of literature. Chandler's iconic books are all about a lone-wolf gumshoe, a knight-errant determined to tilt against the corrupt windmills of big business and powerful government, all the while trying to escape becoming hopelessly entangled with a beautiful blonde, who, ultimately, is nothing but trouble.

Postmortem, by Patricia Cornwell

Whatever you might think about the quality (or lack thereof) of Cornwell's recent works, when her first book debuted in 1990, it was a sensation. *Postmortem* swept the awards lists on both sides of the Atlantic for a reason: it is a frighteningly compelling mystery. Cornwell not only gave readers both an intriguing insider's look at the role of the coroner's office in solving crimes and a conflicted, complex new mystery heroine, but also *Postmortem*'s plot—in which Virginia's chief medical examiner Kay Scarpetta takes on a serial strangler—was scary enough to have us going around and checking to see that all the doors in our homes were locked while we read it.

THREE THINGS TO REMEMBER WHEN WORKING WITH MYSTERY READERS

1. The mystery genre is divided into subgenres: amateur sleuth, private eye, procedurals, and historical sleuths. Some of your patrons will read across the mystery genre, but others will want books from only one subgenre.
2. There is a wide range of graphic violence and language in mysteries. Readers provide us with clues as to how much graphic violence and

language they are comfortable with when they use terms such as *cozy* (no graphic violence or swearing whatsoever), *soft boiled* (some realistic grittiness), *hard boiled* (blood and guts often spill, and characters can curse like teamsters), and *noir* (the world is a bleak and dismal place, and it is only going to get worse tomorrow).

3. Some authors write more than one kind of mystery or even different kinds of books. For example, Susan Wittig Albert writes a contemporary amateur sleuth series featuring herb-shop owner China Bayles and a cozy historical mystery series with Beatrix Potter as a sleuth, and she has just begun a new series set in 1930s Colorado. Sue Grafton's first two books were definitely not mysteries. Robert B. Parker has written three different detective series and more than a couple of westerns. When an author has more than one series, during the readers' advisory chat be sure to clarify with readers which one or ones they want.

AND THE WINNER IS . . .

If you know only one award in the mystery field, it should be the Edgar. Presented annually since 1946 by the Mystery Writers of America, the Edgar is given to mysteries in different categories, such as Best First Mystery, Best Mystery, and Best Mystery Short Story. Different committees made up of MWA members (and thus writers themselves) vote on the Edgars.

4

AMATEUR SLEUTHS
Where's Jessica Fletcher
When You Need Her?

Amateur sleuths have played an important role in the mystery genre ever since Edgar Allan Poe's Chevalier C. Auguste Dupin appeared in 1841. Many Golden Age mystery fiction detectives were amateurs, including Agatha Christie's Miss Marple and Dorothy L. Sayers's Lord Peter Wimsey. Even though writers such as Dashiell Hammett and Raymond Chandler may have dragged murder out of the drawing room and into the mean streets in the 1930s, authors such as Rita Mae Brown and Carolyn Hart prove that murder most domestic is still popular with readers more than a century after it first appeared on the scene.

The draw of the amateur detective for many readers is simple: these sleuths are just like the readers themselves. Amateur sleuths do not have the training or resources of professionals, and so they must rely on their own wits when it comes to solving a crime. Thus, many mystery readers find it easier to relate to someone like Katherine Hall Page's Faith Sibley Fairchild, who has to fit in the occasional bit of detecting with her ongoing, everyday duties as a wife and mother, than Patricia Cornwell's coroner sleuth Kay Scarpetta, whose professional raison d'être involves using her forensic skills to find killers.

Because amateur sleuths are not paid for their detective skills, they must have some compelling reason for becoming involved in an investigation. In some books, the amateur sleuth is the police's leading suspect in a murder investigation and takes up detection to find the real killer (and keep him- or herself out of jail). In other books, a close friend or relative of the amateur detective is the one in danger of being charged, and the protagonist tries to clear the suspect's name. And then there are novels in which the police rule a death to be accidental but the amateur sleuth knows it is really murder, which means it is up to the amateur sleuth to bring the killer to justice.

Amateur sleuths do have some advantages over their professional counterparts. Often, amateur detectives can find out more information than the police from other suspects simply because they are not as intimidating. Amateurs can more easily blend into a community—especially a small town or village—and unearth important tidbits of gossip that professionals fail to discover. Amateur sleuths frequently have personal connections that they can use, and they do not have to play by the same rules as professional detectives.

Amateur sleuths also face a few challenges that other kinds of sleuths don't. For the most part, amateur sleuths do not have any authority to investigate a crime or apprehend a killer. In some cases, a writer will align the amateur sleuth with a professional counterpart, such as a police officer, who can help with these things. Some examples of this kind of partnership include Nancy Pickard's Jenny McCain series and Susan Wittig Albert's China Bayles books.

The amateur sleuth subgenre does have some conventions that writers must follow or risk losing readers. In the amateur sleuth subgenre, the murderer usually comes from within a closed circle of suspects. In other words, the killer is someone the detective already knows, whether a relative, a coworker, or a friend. In most amateur sleuth mysteries there is an absence of the graphic language and realistically detailed violence found in other mystery subgenres, such as private-detective and procedural mysteries. The amateur sleuth subgenre, more so than other mystery subgenres, requires a willing sense of disbelief on the part of the reader. In other words, the reader must be willing to believe that an amateur could become involved in solving a crime, when in reality this would not necessarily be the case.

Creating a willing sense of disbelief in the reader can be challenging for mystery writers, especially those who write an ongoing series. If an author cannot figure out some credible way to introduce murder into an amateur sleuth's life, the writer risks creating a detective who suffers from the dreaded Cabot Cove syndrome (i.e., the highly improbably number of residents who are murdered in the television sleuth Jessica Fletcher's town of Cabot Cove).

Some mystery writers have found a successful solution to this problem by giving their fictional sleuths occupations that move them around the country or that allow them to bring new characters into their sleuths' lives. Lynn Hamilton's books feature the detective Laura McClintock, an antiques dealer whose career takes her around the globe in search of art treasures. Nevada Barr's park-ranger sleuth Anna Pigeon finds herself assigned to a variety of national parks around the country. Other writers give their amateur sleuth a unique occupation, which in turn gives the sleuth a credible reason for getting involved in a murder investigation. One example of this is Emma Lathen, the pseudonym for the economist Mary Jane Latsis and the lawyer Martha B. Hennisart. The two used their knowledge of the world of finance to create banker and sleuth John Putnam Thatcher—because according to the two writers, "there is nothing on God's earth a banker can't get into."

Another example of how an author can overcome this obstacle is Elaine Viets's Dead-End Job series featuring Helen Hawthorne. After an incident with her ex-husband, Rob, makes her a fugitive from the law, Helen is forced to take a series of dead-end jobs—jobs in which employers don't ask a lot of questions but for which the working conditions and pay are terrible—to survive financially. With each book in the series, Viets has Helen working at a different place of employment—a bookstore, a bridal salon, and a country club—which puts her in contact with a new group of people (and potential murder victims).

As you can see, there is incredible diversity in the amateur sleuth subgenre. Whether it is a little-old-lady snoop in sensible shoes who stamps out crime in her village, an amateur detective who uses his or her field of expertise to solve murders that have stumped the pros, or even a four-legged sleuth who helps its "human" put the pieces of a puzzling mystery together, there truly is an amateur sleuth for almost every reader.

KEY AUTHORS: CLASSIC AMATEUR SLEUTHS

During the Golden Age of mystery fiction (from approximately 1920 to 1940), literally hundreds of amateur sleuths made their literary debuts on both sides of the Atlantic. Some, like Lord Peter Wimsey and Miss Marple, have become immortal additions to the mystery canon, whereas others have faded into literary obscurity. Here are our choices for a few classic amateur detectives who will always be in style with readers.

Agatha Christie

For millions of readers, Agatha Christie *is* the mystery genre. For more than five decades, the Queen of Crime devised dozens of devilishly clever ways to commit murder, and more than 2 billion copies of her books have been sold around the world. In addition to writing eighty novels and more than a dozen short-story collections, Christie wrote nineteen plays, including *Mousetrap*, the longest-running play in history. In the mystery genre, Christie's books are the best example of the puzzle-based, traditional mystery, in which readers compete with a fictional sleuth to guess the identity of the killer. Christie almost created an international literary contretemps in 1926, when her book *The Murder of Roger Ackroyd* was published, with many critics and not a few fans crying, "Foul!" Some readers claimed that Christie broke one of the cardinal rules of detective writing at the time (we could say more, but it would spoil the book for you). But with *The Murder of Roger Ackroyd*, the always-clever Christie played by the same fair-play rules of detection in that book that she used throughout her career; she just stretched them to their most creative limits. Although Christie created several different sleuths, she is best known for her characters Hercule Poirot, a former Belgian police commissioner turned private detective, and Jane Marple, an English spinster with a natural gift for solving mysteries. In many ways, Christie's Miss Marple is the quintessential amateur detective. She has no special training or official standing, yet she successfully solved a number of baffling murders in twenty short stories and twelve novels simply using her own knowledge of human nature. She was first introduced in Christie's *Murder at the Vicarage*, in which the detestable Colonel Prothero is found murdered in St. Mary Mead; this book serves as an excellent entry to the Miss Marple style of detection, and Miss Marple is a legendary amateur sleuth who remains the gold standard by which all other spinster sleuths are judged.

NOW READ: Elizabeth Daly

Agatha Christie said that Elizabeth Daly was her favorite American mystery writer, so suggesting Daly's books to Christie's fans seems like a match made in literary heaven, especially because Daly's series featuring Henry Gamadge—who makes a living as a consultant on old books and autographs—not only follow the same set of Golden Age mystery-writing rules that Christie employed but also have the same cleverly constructed plots and civilized settings as those of Christie. Once readers have finished all of Daly's books, they can continue on with five mysteries written by Elizabeth Daly's niece Eleanor Boylan, whose books feature Henry's wife, the now-widowed Clara Gamadge. Readers can begin with *Unexpected Night*, in which Henry has some questions as to whether Amberley Cowden threw himself off a cliff or was helped over the edge.

Dorothy L. Sayers

Dorothy L. (never forget the *L*, as she got quite cranky when people did) Sayers, Christie's main literary rival, introduced one of the most popular amateur sleuths in fiction: Lord Peter Wimsey. An important factor to take into account when working with readers is that Sayers's mysteries differ in tone and style from Christie's works. Sayers was more concerned with writing "literary" mysteries, and her writing is noted for its richly descriptive style. Even though Sayers's books have a more upmarket flavor, she played by the same set of literary detective rules as Christie did. Sayers's mysteries do offer complicated, clever murder plots (sometimes a bit too clever, if you ask us) that challenge the reader to solve the crime, but plot was never really Sayers's forte. Sayers was more interested in developing her characters—and what a cast of characters she created, from Wimsey's uniquely talented manservant Bunter to the mystery writer and romantic foil Harriet Vane—to worry too much about the practicality of her fictional murders. Sayers did create another detective in addition to her aristocratic main sleuth Wimsey in the person of crack traveling wine-and-spirits salesman Montague Egg, who appeared in classic puzzle-based short stories in two different story collections, *In the Teeth of Evidence and Other Mysteries* and *Hangman's Holiday*. Start off readers who are new to Sayers with the first Wimsey book, *Whose Body?*, in which Wimsey is called in to investigate when an architect finds a dead body in his bathtub.

NOW READ: Margery Allingham

Readers who love Dorothy L. Sayers's elegantly written Wimsey books will definitely want to give Margery Allingham's series featuring the aristocratic amateur sleuth Albert Campion a try. Like Sayers, Allingham was as concerned with the literary merits of her writing as she was in following the Golden Age rules for crafting a fair-play puzzle, which means that her books have the same combination of rich characterization, stylish writing, and perplexing crimes. This is a series best read in order, so start with *The Black Dudley Murder*, in which Campion finds out that a weekend in the country can really be murder.

Ellery Queen

The American writer Ellery Queen (actually the pseudonym for Frederic Dannay and Manfred B. Lee, two cousins who wrote together) excelled at writing traditionally crafted, puzzle-based books. Ellery Queen—yes, they named their detective after themselves, or vice versa—became so

popular he was spun off into a long-running radio series, three television series, and several motion pictures, and he even lent his name to a
mystery magazine that continues to be published today. The Ellery Queen
books, especially the earlier titles in the series, such as *The Chinese Orange
Mystery*, are excellent examples of the Golden Age, puzzle-based brand
of crime fiction. Although the early books maintain the lighter tone of
many 1930s and 1940s amateur sleuth series, the series tended to get a bit
darker and grimmer over the decades, as the authors adapted their literary creation to changes going on in the mystery genre itself. Readers new
to Queen will want to begin with *The Roman Hat Mystery*, in which Ellery
and his father try to find out who murdered an obnoxious lawyer in the
middle of a production of a standing-room-only play.

NOW READ: Anthony Berkeley

Readers who enjoy the cleverly constructed plotting of Ellery Queen's
classic mysteries will also want to give Anthony Berkeley's books a try.
Berkeley, a pseudonym for the British author A. B. Cox, also wrote mysteries as Francis Iles and wrote more than a dozen traditional mysteries, most
of which feature mystery writer Roger Sheringham. Although Berkeley
successfully employed many of the Golden Age conventions of the mystery genre—including carefully clued plots and a cast of convenient suspects—in his Sheringham books, he did so with a deliciously dry sense
of wit. *The Poisoned Chocolates Case*, in which a group of society intellectu-
als (including Sheringham) try to determine who sent Sir Eustace a box
of poisoned chocolates, is an excellent introduction to Berkeley's classic
brand of mysteries.

John Dickson Carr

John Dickson Carr became famous as the king of the locked-room mystery, in which readers have to guess not only who dunit but also exactly
how the murder was committed. (In fact, in *The Three Coffins*, Carr's long-
running series, detective Gideon Fell actually delivers a lecture on the various ways to construct a successful locked-room murder!) In addition to
four different series (one featuring bombastic Sir Henry Merrivale, written
under the pseudonym Carter Dickson), Carr wrote a number of different
kinds of books, including several time-travel tales, a few historical mysteries, and a couple of subtle supernatural suspense novels (you might say
he was ahead of the literary curve on the whole genre-blending thing),
but his traditional, clue-based mysteries continue to be an excellent choice

for fans of classically constructed, devilishly clever detective fiction. For an idea of the flavor of Carr's books, try *Hag's Nook*, in which Gideon Fell investigates when Martin Starbeth, the last surviving male heir to the Starbeth fortune, is found dead after spending time at Hag's Nook, an old gallows in an abandoned prison.

NOW READ: G. K. Chesterton

Readers who have gobbled up everything by John Dickson Carr can be steered toward G. K. Chesterton, Carr's own favorite writer and the creator of one of the genre's most unlikely sleuths: Father Brown. In addition to their fiendishly clever plots, many of Carr's mysteries have a touch of the supernatural about them, and Chesterton's Father Brown mysteries have the same seemingly impossible-to-solve plots (including several locked-room stories) with a dash of the mystical. Start with *The Innocence of Father Brown*, a sterling collection of short stories featuring the unassuming religious sleuth with an umbrella, who uses his mind, his heart, and his soul to solve crimes.

KEY AUTHORS: MODERN-DAY AMATEUR DETECTIVES

Although you might think the traditional amateur sleuth went out of style with the rotary-dial telephone (and if you have to ask what that is, we give up!), the truth is that ever since the 1980s, there has been a renaissance of amateur snoops—from Miss Marple wannabes to glamorous twenty-something sleuths—each of whom definitely gives Ellery or Lord Peter a run for their money.

Carolyn Hart

Carolyn G. Hart is the author of several different mystery series and stand-alone novels, including her long-running, award-winning books featuring bookstore owner and amateur sleuth Annie Laurance Darling. With these books, Hart skillfully takes the best elements of the traditional Golden Age mystery (including a carefully crafted, puzzling plot) and successfully translates it into a contemporary setting. Not only do her Annie Laurance Darling books, which began with *Death on Demand*, have the kind of engaging protagonist and realistically quirky cast of secondary characters that modern mystery readers demand, but Hart also thoughtfully provides many references to old and new mystery writers in her books, which are guaranteed to delight readers and have them search-ing for those books, too. In particular, Hart's *The Christie Caper* has Annie searching for a clever killer who is attending a centenary celebration in honor of Agatha Christie, which also gives Hart the opportunity to extol the literary virtues of Christie's mysteries. Hart has written other books (including one series featuring retired journalist and current amateur sleuth Henrietta "Henrie O" O'Dwyer Collins, and another with ghostly amateur detective Bailey Ruth Raeburn), but the two common threads neatly tying together all of Hart's work together are her ability to create memorable amateur sleuths and her love of the mystery genre. An excel-lent starting point for most readers who are new to Hart is her first Annie Laurance Darling book, *Death on Demand*, in which Annie meets her future husband, Max, while trying to figure out who killed the mystery writer Elliot Morgan.

NOW READ: Gillian Roberts

Mystery readers who enjoy the strong romantic subplot woven into Caroline Hart's Annie Laurance Darling mysteries and their bookish fla-vor will definitely want to give Gillian Roberts's Amanda Pepper books a try. Beginning with the first book in the series, Amanda, a teacher at an exclusive and expensive private high school in Philadelphia, finds herself becoming professionally and personally involved with homicide detective C. K. Mackenzie. With many of the Amanda Pepper mysteries, readers will also find a reference to some great work of literature cleverly worked into the plot, be it *Lady Macbeth* in *Caught Dead in Philadelphia* or *The Picture of Dorian Gray* in *With Friends Like These* . . . . Start readers off with *Caught Dead in Philadelphia*, in which Amanda's bad day at work only gets worse when she arrives home and finds a coworker's dead body behind her sofa.

Dorothy Cannell

Dorothy Cannell's first book featuring Ellie Simons and Bentley T. Haskell, *The Thin Woman*, is a classic in the mystery genre (and one of our favorite mysteries of all time). *The Thin Woman* really can't be beat for its winning combination of wicked wit and charm, and all of Cannell's mysteries are wonderfully fun and quite amusing reads. Cannell's characters can be a bit wacky—especially her secondary characters—but that just adds to the charm of her stories. In many ways, Cannell's mysteries are a modern update of the humorous detective fiction written by classic authors such as Phoebe Atwood Taylor and Craig Rice, mysteries in which laughter is as important to the plot as detection. Give readers *The Thin Woman*, in which an overweight and overwrought Ellie must lose sixty-three pounds (and Bentley must write a book without a word of smut in it) to inherit her late uncle's estate, and they will soon be fans of Cannell's madcap mysteries.

NOW READ: Donna Andrews

Readers who have become addicted to Dorothy Cannell's entertaining mix of mirth and murder will want to give a try to Donna Andrews's humorous mysteries featuring the blacksmith, sculptor, and reluctant amateur sleuth Meg Langslow. Andrews's Langslow books offer the same irresistible combination of quirky characters, laughter-laced writing, and soupçon of romance that make Cannell's books such an irresistible literary treat. Begin with *Murder with Peacocks*, which introduces readers to Meg, who never thought her duties as bridesmaid in three different weddings would also involve finding out who killed an extremely annoying out-of-town guest.

Katherine Hall Page

Katherine Hall Page's series sleuth is wife, mother, caterer, and amateur snoop Faith Sibley Fairchild, and her mysteries, beginning with *The Body in the Belfry*, have the same entertaining mix of well-plotted mysteries and captivating characters that amateur sleuth readers love. By cleverly making her heroine a caterer, Page not only gets to include a sampling of delicious recipes in each book but also gives her fictional sleuth a believable entrée into any number of social circles. Although Page writes a contemporary amateur sleuth series, she hasn't forgotten her subgenre's literary roots. All of the Fairchild books are classically constructed murder mysteries with a convincing cast of suspects and clue-rich plots. In fact, with *The Body in the Ivy*, Page even uses Christie's quintessential suspense novel *And Then There Were None* as a wonderful source of literary inspiration for her own intriguing story about a group of women who first meet in college and decades later find themselves invited to a private reunion on an isolated island. All of Page's books are terrific, but start with *The Body in the Belfry*, in which Fairchild really gets to know her new neighbors when she stumbles across the body of a beautiful blackmailer in the church's belfry.

NOW READ: Karen MacInerney

After readers have caught up with all of Faith Fairchild's adventures in detection, send them on to Karen MacInerney for a similar feast of cozy crime solving. MacInerney's Gray Whale Inn series stars Natalie Barnes, who leaves behind her old life in Texas and moves to Cranberry Island, Maine. There Natalie juggles the daily demands of running the Gray Whale, her bed-and-breakfast, while solving a surprising number of murders that occur on the small island. MacInerney delivers the same irresistible mix of engaging characters, traditionally plotted mysteries, and a generous helping of delicious recipes as in Page's books. Start with the first in the series, *Murder on the Rocks*, in which a murderer nearly succeeds in putting new innkeeper Natalie out of business for good.

Margaret Maron

Margaret Maron got her literary start writing short stories in the late 1960s and early 1970s. Her first detective series featured NYPD lieutenant Sigrid Harald, who debuted in 1981 in *One Coffee With*. In 1992, Maron begin her award-winning mysteries starring North Carolina district judge and amateur detective Deborah Knott with *Bootlegger's Daughter*. Not only are the Knott books well-plotted, traditional mysteries, but Knott's job as a traveling judge takes her to various courts around North Carolina, which provides Maron with the opportunity to write about a place she truly loves. Maron actually starts with a setting and then builds her story for Knott around that specific locale. Many of North Carolina's noted industries and crafts, such as furniture and pottery, also play a role in the plot of Maron's Knott books. Although Maron does write a very traditional amateur sleuth series, she does not hesitate to bring the amateur sleuth subgenre into the twenty-first century by including contemporary issues such as racism, immigration, and land development in her impeccably crafted plots. Start with *Bootlegger's Daughter*, in which attorney Deborah Knott juggles running for district judge with her own investigation into a murder that occurred eighteen years earlier.

NOW READ: Barbara Neely

Readers who treasure the same complex and complicated characters, strong sense of place, and willingness to incorporate tough social issues into a traditional mystery plot as in Margaret Maron's Deborah Knott series will want to add Barbara Neely's award-winning series featuring African American domestic worker Blanche White to their must-read lists.

With her own estimable sense of grace, a generous measure of true grit, and a dry sense of humor, Blanche has cleaned up crime in four books to date. Start with her literary debut, *Blanche on the Lam,* in which Blanche's own past as a check kiter forces her to take a maid's job with a wealthy Southern family who is moving to their country home for a week.

KEY AUTHORS: FOUR-LEGGED AMATEUR SLEUTHS

These days there is a veritable pack of dog- and cat-owning sleuths, all of whom seem to owe their success in detection to their furry counterparts. If your reader wants an entertaining mystery centered on a four-legged detective, try one of these authors.

Lilian Jackson Braun

The idea that an animal can solve a mystery might seem far fetched, but former journalist turned novelist Lilian Jackson Braun not only proved it is possible but also hit the best-seller lists for two decades while doing so. Braun's books represent yet another aspect of the amateur sleuth subgenre: the sleuth with a pet who subtly (or not) plays a role in the investigation. In her gently humorous Cat Who . . . series, Braun's series sleuth, the newspaper reporter Jim Qwilleran, receives unexpected help with his amateur detective duties from his two Siamese cats, Koko and Yum Yum, who frequently provide the vital clue needed to solve the mystery. In her books (the titles of which all begin *The Cat Who . . .*) Braun combines an ongoing cast of regular characters; a cozy, almost old-fashioned mystery, usually set in the fictional town of Pickax in Moose County; and a dash of romance into a comfortable amateur sleuth series that lasted almost four decades and continues to remain popular with readers today. The best place to start is Braun's first book, *The Cat Who Could Read Backwards,* in which Qwilleran doesn't realize that spunky Siamese cat Koko is actually helping him investigate the murder of a snobby art critic.

NOW READ: Shirley Rousseau Murphy

If readers in your library find the idea of sleuthing felines to be simply catnip, once they have finished up with Lilian Jackson Braun's series, steer them toward the Joe Grey mysteries written by Shirley Rousseau Murphy. Set in the fictional California town of Molena Point, the books star the feline sleuth Joe Grey and his two partners-in-detection, Dulcie and Kit. The tone of the series is a bit less cozy than the Cat Who . . . books, but Murphy offers the same ongoing, engaging cast of characters and cat sleuths, who not only take an active role in detection, as in Braun's mysteries, but also can communicate with select humans. Begin with the first book, *Cat on the Edge*, which introduces Joe, who after an accident gains the ability to understand and speak to humans, and uses his new gifts to take on a case of murder.

Rita Mae Brown

Other amateur detective series with animals include Emmy-nominated screenwriter, poet, and social critic Rita Mae Brown's wonderfully charming series with postmistress Mary Minor "Harry" Harristeen and her cosleuths: her cat, Mrs. Murphy, and her Welsh corgi, Tee Tucker, whose adventures in detection begin with *Wish You Were Here*. Brown actually credits her own cat, Sneaky Pie Brown, as the coauthor of the series, and the books are rich in cozy Southern atmosphere and realistically quirky characters. In many ways, the Mrs. Murphy mysteries are as much character-rich novels of manners as they are mysteries. Brown also writes another animal-based amateur sleuth series featuring Sister Jane, a Virginia-based master of the hunt, and she just debuted yet another four-legged detective in *A Nose for Justice*, in which canines King and Baxter help Nevada rancher Jeep Reed solve a puzzling murder. To get a good idea of the flavor of Brown's mysteries, try *Wish You Were Here*, in which the postmistress Harristeen gradually comes to realize that seemingly pleasant postcards coming through her post office are really death threats.

NOW READ: Suzette A. Hill

Readers who enjoy they way in which Rita Mae Brown gives her fictional four-legged sleuths and active (and vocal) role in crime solving will want to give Suzette A. Hill's books a try. Hill's series features Reverend Francis Oughterard, or F. O., as he is known, and his sarcastic cat, Maurice, and lovable but less-than-sharp-witted dog Bouncer, each of whom has a turn in narrating the story. Hill's series offers readers the same cozy, small-town (well, OK, small-village) setting found in Brown's books, along with an infectious mix of whimsy and detection. Begin with Hill's debut book, *A Load of Old Bones*, in which Maurice and Bouncer try to help clear F. O. from the charge that he murdered a parishioner.

Susan Conant

As a six-time winner of the Dog Writers Association of America's Maxwell Medallion award, Susan Conant has proved that she knows a thing or two about dogs, and her series featuring *Dog's Life* columnist and dog trainer Holly Winters are filled with intriguing details about canines in addition to being entertaining mysteries. Along with her two Alaskan malamute dogs, Holly finds herself stuck in the role of amateur detective on a regular basis as she stumbles across murders in veterinarians' offices, pet shops, dog retreats, and dog shows. In addition to her Dog Lovers mysteries, Conant gives felines a chance at mystery solving with her book *Scratch the Surface*, in which a mystery writer whose books feature cats but who ironically knows nothing about them finds a cold corpse of a strange man and a live cat left in her home. To begin with, we suggest *A New Leash on Death*, in which Holly finds that Rowdy, an orphaned malamute from an obedience class, is a great help in digging up clues as to who murdered his owner.

NOW READ: Laurien Berenson

Laurien Berenson knows canines. Her grandmother showed terriers and was a dog-show judge herself, and her mother also bred and showed terriers. A real-life dog-napping case that Berenson was covering for the *New York Times* became the inspiration for her first mystery featuring Melanie Travis, a journalist who quickly finds her life going to the dogs. As does Conant, Berenson offers readers solidly constructed, puzzling mysteries set in the vividly detailed world of dog training and dog shows. Start with Melanie's first fiction case, *A Pedigree to Die For*, in which Melanie's Aunt Peg asks her to do some sleuthing when her Uncle Max, a breeder of championship poodles, is found dead on the kennel floor.

KEY AUTHORS: CRAFTY OR CULINARY AMATEUR SNOOPS

Giving an amateur sleuth a pet as a partner-in-crime is not the only way some authors have tried to set their series apart from the literary pack. The current trend in amateur sleuth mysteries is for the protagonist to have a crafty job or hobby. From gardening and candle making to quilting and cooking, there really is an amateur sleuth series for every pastime.

Susan Wittig Albert

Most authors consider themselves fortunate if they come up with one successful amateur sleuth. Award-winning Susan Wittig Albert has four different series to her credit. Albert, a former university administrator, actually wrote a number of different books under several pseudonyms before she published her first novel featuring China Bayles, a Houston lawyer who gives up her law practice to open an herb shop in the small town of Pecan Springs. Along the way, China meets former police detective Mike McQuaid, who not only helps with several of China's cases but becomes an important person in her domestic life as well. Each title in the China Bayles series is tied to a particular herb, and Albert not only cleverly sows the herb into the plot but also provides useful instructions on growing and using the herb. In fact, Albert also wrote a gardening and cooking companion book to the China Bayles books as a result of reader demand. In addition to her China Bayles books, Albert, writing as Robin Paige, with her husband, Bill, authored a historical mystery series set in Victorian England featuring author Kate Ardleigh and Charles Sheridan in an ongoing cozy amateur sleuth series with Beatrix Potter as a detective (well, she gets some help from her animal friends), and she has authored a new series set in 1930s Colorado with an older group of female amateur sleuths. Those new to Albert should begin with *Thyme of Death*, in which China Bayles decides to investigate when a friend who is suffering from cancer "commits suicide."

NOW READ: Sheila Connolly

Just like China Bayles, Meg Corey, the amateur sleuth in Sheila Connolly's new series, left her old life behind to start fresh in a new place. After being jilted by her boyfriend and downsized at work, Meg leaves Boston for the small town of Grandford, Massachusetts, where her mother has inherited the family's old apple orchard. As Meg works to restore the colonial home and bring the orchard back into production, she finds herself frequently taking on the role of amateur sleuth as well. Readers who start with the first in the series, *One Bad Apple*, will find that Connolly delivers not only a strong cast of secondary characters and ongoing romantic subplot, as in Albert's China Bayles books, but also some fun and fascinating details about apple growing.

Earlene Fowler

Earlene Fowler not only gives her amateur detective and quilter Benni Harper a job in a folk-art museum but also uses the names of quilts for each of her books, starting with Benni's first sleuthing attempts in *Fool's Puzzle*. To avoid boring herself, and any possible readers of her books, Fowler decided to include everything she herself loved—a strong female protagonist, a vivid sense of place, and an entertaining plot centered on quilting—in *Fool's Puzzle* and the successive books in the series. Several of the characters in the series were inspired by some of Fowler's own female relatives who were born and raised on farms or ranches, and by others who were talented quilters or needlewomen. Fowler translated these real-life ladies into the realistically complex characters that have become a key appeal factor of the Benni Harper series. For a good idea of the flavor of Fowler's writing, start with *Fool's Puzzle*, in which the recently widowed Benni decides to investigate when an artist is found dead in the San Celina Folk Art Museum.

NOW READ: Elizabeth Lynn Casey

The strong sense of family, friends, and community (and subtle, yet important romance) woven into Earlene Fowler's Benni Harper mysteries is also a key component in Elizabeth Lynn Casey's series featuring Tori Sinclair. After moving to the small Southern town of Sweet Briar, South Carolina, to take a job as the town librarian, Tori worries that she will have trouble fitting in—especially because she is a Yankee. Fortunately, the ladies of the local sewing circle adopt Tori as one of their own, and their support and friendship help her build a new life. Start readers with the first in the series, *Sew Deadly*, in which Tori's first week on the new job hits a low point after she stumbles across a dead body in the library.

Maggie Sefton

Knitting is the common thread that stitches together all of Maggie Sefton's books featuring the amateur sleuth Kelly Flynn. In *Knit One, Kill Two*, Sefton introduces readers to Kelly, who leaves her job as an accountant in Washington, D.C., to travel to the small town of Fort Connor, Colorado, when her aunt is murdered. Flynn not only gains a new circle of friends after meeting the local knitting group but also eventually embarks on a new career after she takes over her aunt's knitting shop, House of Lambspun. Sefton's Kelly Flynn series is an excellent example of how many crafty mysteries can appeal to two different readerships. Sefton includes numerous details about yarn—from raising alpacas to spinning their wool and dying the fiber—in the series, and she even includes patterns for various knitting projects in each book, which means that her colorful titles are a hit with both mystery readers and those involved in the art and craft of knitting. Because Sefton's books are better when read in order, start off readers who are new to Sefton with *Knit One, Kill Two*.

NOW READ: Monica Ferris

Readers searching for the same cozy sense of small-town community and crafty mystery plots found in Sefton's books will want to snap up Monica Ferris's mysteries featuring Betsy Devonshire. In addition to delivering the requisite cast of strong supporting characters, Ferris embroiders her neatly stitched Betsy Devonshire mysteries with a generous dash of needle-sharp wit. Start with *Crewel World*, in which Betsy arrives in Excelsior, Minnesota, to visit her sister Margot, the owner of a local needlecraft shop, only to find the visit cut short when Margot is found murdered.

Diane Mott Davidson

There are at least a baker's dozen of mystery writers cooking up culinary-flavored crimes, but for many mystery readers, Diane Mott Davidson is the top literary chef. Davidson, whose Colorado caterer and amateur sleuth Goldy Bear Schulz continually seems to be involved in some murder investigation, didn't initially set out to write a culinary mystery, but after working on her first novel, her critique group informed her that one of the secondary characters in the novel was taking over the plot. So Davidson reworked the story, moving the caterer into the protagonist's slot, and a new amateur sleuth star was born. The owner of Goldilocks' Catering (where everything is just right!), Goldy lives in a small town with her son and has a realistically complicated past (including an abusive ex-husband). As the series progresses, Goldy's ex makes a few appearances, and Goldy finds a new romantic partner in the Aspen Meadows sheriff's investigator Tom Schulz, which gives the books their strong realistic flavor. Although Davidson may have perfected the recipe for the ideal murder mystery, she is equally dedicated to coming up with tasty new recipes for each book, and her Goldy Bear books consistently satisfy both mystery readers and cooks. To get a good taste of Davidson's writing, start with *Catering to Nobody*, in which Goldy's former father-in-law is nearly killed after drinking poisoned lemonade served at an event she catered.

NOW READ: Laura Childs

Childs currently writes three different cozy craft- and culinary-inspired mystery series, but we think her books featuring Theodosia "Theo" Browning, owner of Indigo Tea Shop in Charleston, South Carolina, are an excellent suggestion for readers who have devoured Diane Mott Davidson's books. Childs serves up the same tempting mix of traditionally plotted mysteries, engaging characters, and mouthwatering recipes found in the Goldy Bear Schulz series, and she excels at incorporating the rich historical flavor of the series's Charleston setting into each book. Start with *Death by Darjeeling*, in which Theo takes on the new job of amateur sleuth when a guest is found murdered at the historical-homes garden party she is catering.

Joanne Fluke

Joanne Fluke has written a number of books under her own name and under various pseudonyms, but it is her cozy culinary series featuring Hannah Swensen for which she is best known and loved by readers. The series begins with *The Chocolate Chip Cookie Murder*, in which Hannah decides to open her own bakery in her small Minnesota hometown. As the series progresses, Fluke stirs in a dash of romance in the form of police detective Mike Kingston, who frequently finds himself partnering with Hannah to solve the murder. It might seem as if Hannah spends more time solving mysteries than she does actually baking up treats in her shop, but food definitely remains the focus of this series. Fluke has devised dozens of culinary-inspired plots, and she spends as much time developing and including at least a dozen different recipes in each book. To start off your Fluke-inspired literary meal, choose *The Chocolate Chip Cookie Murder*, in which Hannah discovers she has a talent not only for baking but also for detective work when she decides to find out who left the body of the Cozy Cow Dairy deliveryman behind her shop.

NOW READ: Claudia Bishop
Claudia Bishop is the pseudonym for the science-fiction writer Mary Stanton, who has also authored several amateur sleuth series, including one featuring Sarah Quilliam and her sister Meg. Sarah (or Quill, as everyone calls her) is the owner of a small inn in Hemlock Falls, New York, where her sister and co-owner Meg works as the chef. Bishop's Hemlock Falls series offers many of the same ingredients found in Fluke's books, including a cozy, small-town setting; an engaging cast of quirky secondary characters; some tempting recipes; and a bit of romance. Start your readers with the first in the series, *A Taste for Murder*, in which Quill and Meg feel compelled to investigate when one of their guests is found dead at the annual Hemlock Falls History Days festival.

KEY AUTHORS: AMATEUR SLEUTHS
WITH A PROFESSIONAL EDGE

For readers who want a good mystery with intriguing details about some fascinating field of study or unusual occupation, there are a number of amateur sleuth mysteries in which an author's own expertise effectively becomes the driving force for writing a series.

Dick Francis

For many readers Dick Francis is the mystery author who writes about horses. It is certainly true that Francis used his experiences as a steeple-chase jockey in England as inspiration for a number of best-selling mysteries set in the world of professional horse racing, thus proving that writing what you know can pay off. But there is more to Francis than just detective novels featuring murder at the racetrack. With their often darker and occasionally grittier tone, Francis's books are an important addition to the amateur sleuth subgenre, because they demonstrate that not all amateur sleuth series have to be cozy. In addition, Francis's books are an excellent example of that fact that many readers enjoy learning something new while reading for pleasure. Francis's mysteries almost always offer some fascinating insider details about the world of horse racing, including his first book *Dead-Cert*, in which jockey Alan York discovers that a champion steeplechase rider's death on the track was no accident, and *Odds Against*, which introduced his one-series character Sid Halley. Francis also branched out into other fields beside horse racing, including wine importing in his book *Proof* and the world of high finance in *Banker*. Because most of Francis's books—with the exception of his Sid Halley titles—are stand-alone mysteries rather than part of a connected series, readers really can start with any of his novels, but if they need a suggestion, we recommend *Odds Against*, in which after being sidelined from his racing career by a hard fall, Sid takes a job with a detective agency.

NOW READ: Jonathan Gash

Although Dick Francis has become famous as the author of horse mysteries, Jonathan Gash is equally well known as the writer of antique detective stories. Gash's series featuring rogue and antique dealer Lovejoy offers readers the same appeal Francis's books do: the opportunity to learn more about some intriguing field of interest in the context of a well-plotted mystery. Like Francis's mysteries, Gash's Lovejoy books are an excellent example of the noncozy amateur sleuth, and much of the fun in the series comes from the charmingly self-preserving Lovejoy, who dispenses a wealth of fascinating details about antiques and forgeries (subjects in which he is well versed). Begin your introduction to this rakish sleuth with *The Judas Pair*, in which Lovejoy is hired to track down a legendary pair of eighteenth-century dueling pistols.

Aaron Elkins

When Aaron Elkins set out to write his first mystery—mainly because the grant funding his teaching career in Europe had run out—he eventually took his wife's advice and based his fictional detective, anthropology professor Gideon Oliver, on himself. In his first mystery, *Fellowship of Fear*, Elkins threw in some bits about how Gideon used his anthropology training to identify the victim from just a few small remains of bones, but Elkins never thought that would become his hook in the crowded amateur sleuth field. Much to Elkin's surprise, readers loved learning how Oliver, a.k.a. the Skeleton Detective, uses his forensic anthropology skills to solve crimes, and Elkins found a new use for his academic training. Since his first mystery debuted, Elkins has gone on to write a series of golfing mysteries with his wife, Charlotte; another series featuring art curator Chris Norgren; and several stand-alone suspense novels—but if we had to suggest just one book of his to read, it would be his Edgar Award–winning *Old Bones*, in which Gideon travels to France to investigate the discovery of human bones from the 1940s that might be tied to the recent deaths in a prominent family in Brittany.

NOW READ: Lyn Hamilton

Readers who have become addicted to the globe-trotting adventures of amateur sleuth Gideon Oliver will want to add Lyn Hamilton to their to-read lists. Just as Aaron Elkins was inspired by his own academic training in anthropology when it came time to create his fictional sleuth, Hamilton used her own extensive travel experiences and knowledge of art and artifacts as the foundation for her amateur detective: Toronto-based antiques dealer Lara McClintoch. Hamilton's books deliver the same compelling mix of vividly detailed locales and intriguing facts about a captivating subject matter found in Elkin's books. Begin readers with *The Xibalba Murders*, in which Lara travels to Mexico to help an old friend, Dr. Castillo, who is soon found murdered.

John Dunning

John Dunning has written a few series and stand-alone mysteries, but he found the perfect setting—the world of rare books—for an amateur sleuth when he created Cliff Janeway, a former Denver policeman turned rare-books dealer. With his Janeway books, Dunning delivers a complex and contemplative protagonist, engaging writing, and compelling plots, but it is Dunning's ability to evoke the world of books and book collecting with such command that readers remember best. Dunning is so skilled at writing about books, that when his first Janeway novel, *Booked to Die*, was published in 1992, it is said to have inspired a subsequent real-life boom in collecting mystery books. Readers new to Dunning's books will want to start with *Booked to Die*, in which after quitting the police force and opening a bookstore, Cliff Janeway finds himself playing detective again when a book scout is murdered.

NOW READ: Lawrence Block

Although Lawrence Block's fictional sleuth Bernie Rhodenbarr didn't start out as a bookseller—his real vocation is thief—by the third book in the series, *The Burglar Who Liked to Quote Kipling*, he has acquired a legitimate profession: used bookstore owner, which make Block's Bernie Rhodenbarr books a nice segue for readers who have finished Dunning's Janeway mysteries and want more mysteries set in the world of collectibles. Throughout the series, Bernie finds his old professional skills coming in handy as he is called on to "retrieve" a number of different valuable items, including coins, paintings, and baseball cards. This also provides the opportunity for readers to learn a bit more about these collectibles, much like readers of Dunning's mysteries learn more about rare books in his Cliff Janeway series. Begin with *The Burglar Who Liked to Quote Kipling*, in which after stealing the only copy of a rare work by Kipling, Bernie finds himself entangled in a murder case.

Nevada Barr

Nevada Barr's series sleuth Anna Pigeon is a professional—a park ranger—but when it comes to solving the murders, Anna retains her amateur status beginning with her first book, *Track of the Cat*. Barr, who was named after the state in which she was born, began her working career as an actress, but when her former husband joined the Park Service, Barr followed him. What many mystery readers love most about Barr's books is how brilliantly she uses different national parks as settings for her stories and how much they, as readers, learn about those places. Setting is actually the first thing that inspires Barr as a writer, and whether it is cliff villages in the Southwest, the cold waters of the Great Lakes region, or even the urban wildness of the Statue of Liberty, all of Barr's Pigeon books have a wonderfully vivid sense of place. To get a good idea of the literary feel of Barr's books, start with *Track of the Cat*, in which Nevada begins to wonder whether the park ranger found in the Guadalupe Mountains of Texas was really killed by a mountain lion.

NOW READ: Sandi Ault

Just as Nevada Barr's Anna Pigeon finds dead bodies an occupational hazard of work, so does Sandi Ault's new addition to the amateur sleuth subgenre: Bureau of Land Management agent Jamaica Wild. Like Barr's mysteries, Ault's Jamaica Wild books are a bit more realistically gritty than the average cozy amateur sleuth series, and Ault is equally skilled at evoking the same strong sense of place (in Ault's case, the desert Southwest) found in Barr's books. In addition, Ault's mysteries are a good read-alike possibility for detective-fiction fans who enjoy strong female sleuths with a knack for solving crimes. Start with the first book in the series, *Wild Indigo*, in which Jamaica, while studying Pueblo culture with Momma Anna Jerome, finds herself taking on the role of sleuth when Momma's son is killed in a buffalo stampede.

5

PRIVATE INVESTIGATORS
Well-Worn Trench Coats, Smoking Gats, and Deadly Dames

Completely unique, instantly recognizable, and absolutely distinctive, the private investigator novel has proved a popular and durable mystery subgenre. What makes a PI novel work? It's the appeal of the underdog, to whom the private investigators are drawn to help, sometimes in spite of their best instincts. It's the attraction of the average Dick or Jane, who, despite of his or her sense of disillusionment or cynicism, is still willing to delve into society's seamy underside to discover the truth. It's the fascination of the paladin, who might wear slightly dented armor but is still willing to tilt against the windmills of big business, graft, and corruption. Raymond Chandler, one of the masters of PI fiction, summed up the appeal of the subgenre best when he wrote in his essay "The Simple Art of Murder" that "down these mean streets a man must go who is not himself mean, who is neither tarnished nor afraid."[1]

The earliest popular PI in fiction is most likely Sir Arthur Conan Doyle's Sherlock Holmes. Although Holmes is sometimes considered an amateur detective, the reality is that he was almost always paid for his work, which makes him the classic private eye—at least according to the Private Eye Writers of America, who define a private investigator as "a person paid for investigative services, but who is not employed by a unit of the government."[2] The popularity of Doyle's detective created a rush of similar sleuths, most of whom were fairly forgettable, but with the arrival of pulp magazines in the 1920s and 1930s, the private-eye subgenre was truly born. Today, the private detective is often considered America's contribution to the world of crime fiction.

There are some common elements found in almost every private-eye novel, key ingredients that readers expect from these mysteries. The private detective, unlike his or her amateur sleuth counterpart, is usually a solitary figure, even a loner at times. Although most private eyes travel this world alone, some detectives do have a trusted sidekick or assistant whom they allow into their world. Two good examples of this are Archie Goodwin, who acts as Nero Wolfe's legman in Rex Stout's books, and Hawk, who acts as enforcer for Robert Parker's Spenser. Private detectives may have a judicial or law enforcement background, but they often have an antagonistic relationship with the courts and the police, another reason for their solitary search for the truth. Although a private eye accepts cases for a fee, often altruistic or idealistic elements compel him or her to finish the work. Private-eye fiction is commonly told in the first person. In other words, the reader experiences events from the point of view of the detective.

The common perception is that the private-eye subgenre is completely dedicated to hard-boiled male detectives, but the truth of the matter is that there is a considerable range in tone—from dark and intense to light and almost humorous—and a diversity of sleuths in this subgenre. Robert B. Parker updated the classic 1930s gumshoe when he created Spenser, PI, a tough but sensitive private detective who is always willing to accept help from his lover Susan, a sophisticated and educated woman. Sandra Scoppettone proved that ladies could be equally as strong as men when she wrote five groundbreaking novels featuring hard-boiled lesbian sleuth Lauren Laurano. S. J. Rozan gives readers two distinct private detectives who work effectively as a team: the Chinese American Lydia Chin and the classic male private investigator Bill Smith. Then there is Vincent Rubio, Eric Garcia's private detective, who is as tough as they come, in part because he is a dinosaur (really!) living in a human's world. Tarquin Hall's colorful new series featuring Vish Puri, owner and founder of Delhi's Most Private Investigations, is both humorous and heartwarming, and its tone is closer to cozy than hard boiled. And with *The Highly Effective Detective*, which introduces Theodore "Teddy" Ruzak, whose first official case is tracking down the hit-and-run driver who killed a gaggle of geese, Richard Yancey cleverly spoofs all of the classic private-eye elements with great wit and charm. These authors and titles are just a few examples of the diversity of choices that can be found in the private eye subgenre.

KEY AUTHORS: CLASSIC PRIVATE EYES

With so many gumshoes from which to choose, where do you start? We suggest beginning at the beginning, so to speak, with four authors who, even if they didn't invent the concept of a private detective, are definitely the subgenre's founding fathers.

Dashiell Hammett

If there is a godfather of the private-eye subgenre, it would have to be Dashiell Hammett. Using his own experiences working as an agent for the Pinkerton National Detective Agency, Hammett wrote short stories for the *Black Mask*, the most famous of the pulp magazines of the 1920s. His stories featuring the Continental Op have all the classic private-eye ingredients, including a first-person narrative, a tough-guy protagonist, and stories set in a realistically gritty and violent world. Hammett is responsible for writing the quintessential private-eye novel of all time (and the source for one of the most unforgettable films of the twentieth century), *The Maltese Falcon*, in which private detective Sam Spade gets tangled up with a variety of shady characters and dangerous dames while searching for person who murdered his partner. Although Hammett is best known for creating Spade and the Continental Op, he is also the author of another, completely different mystery classic, *The Thin Man*, a witty and sharp amateur sleuth story featuring a hard-drinking husband-and-wife team of amateur detectives, who were rumored to have been based on Hammett's own real-life relationship with playwright Lillian Hellman.

NOW READ: Bill Pronzini

Bill Pronzini's series featuring Nameless Detective takes the best elements of the classic PI novel as written by Dashiell Hammett and successfully updates them for today's mystery readers. Like Hammett, Pronzini brings a bit of real-world experience (in Pronzini's case, a job with the U.S. Marshall's office) to his writing, and like Hammett's Continental Op, Nameless's case are most often set in a noir-infused San Francisco. In addition, Pronzini uses the traditional first-person point of view, his writing is concise but vivid, and his action-driven plots evoke Hammett at his best. But Pronzini also brings a much-appreciated dose of pragmatism to the old-fashioned PI school of mystery fiction by making Nameless a more realistic detective, someone who ages and changes over the more than three decades he has spent closing cases. You can begin the series with *The Snatch*, which introduces Nameless, but we think the Shamus Award–winning *Hoodwink*, in which Nameless attends a pulp magazine convention and solves a locked-room murder, is an even better introduction to this terrific, timeless series.

Raymond Chandler

If Hammett is the godfather of the private-eye subgenre, Raymond Chandler is its poet, proving that pulp fiction can also be great literature. In his novels featuring private eye Philip Marlowe, Chandler, who also wrote screenplays in Hollywood, brings an understated subtlety, a rare ability to evoke a strong sense of place and time, and a distinctive dry wit to the subgenre, and he uses those elements to great effect when describing Marlowe's ongoing battle against crime and corruption in the booming city of Los Angeles of the 1930s and 1940s. Although Marlowe might share the classic distrust of authority figures displayed by all hard-boiled detectives, he is a complex man with his own code of conduct, a tough guy with a conscience, a hard-edged realist who is also an idealistic romantic. In so many ways Marlowe is the quintessential private eye: a twentieth-century version of a medieval knight, someone who is continually jousting against the forces of darkness in his world. Start readers off with *The Big Sleep*, in which Marlowe is hired to investigate a case of blackmail and becomes caught up in a web of deceit and murder.

NOW READ: Ross Macdonald

Ross Macdonald, the pseudonym for Kenneth Millar, is considered the literary heir to Raymond Chandler, and it is easy to understand why after reading Macdonald's series featuring private investigator Lew Archer. Many of the Archer books are set in and around Santa Teresa (Macdonald's fictionalized version of Santa Barbara, California), and Macdonald is as gifted as Chandler at making the most of the noirish qualities of sunny California. Macdonald's characters, like Chandler's, have nuance and depth and are all the more real to readers for their flaws. But most of all, in their writing, both Chandler and Macdonald have proved that a great detective story can also be great literature. Begin with the first in the series, *The Moving Target*, in which Elaine Sampson hires Archer to find her missing millionaire husband, Ralph.

Mickey Spillane

Mickey Spillane is the creator of New York City private eye Mike Hammer, a tough-guy avenger with a short-fuse temper and a comic-bookishly violent (but effective) way of dealing with injustice. Beginning with his first book, *I, the Jury*, published in 1947, Spillane turned up the volume in the private-eye subgenre with his brutal and sexy stories featuring Hammer and his ever-faithful secretary (and a private eye herself) Velda. Spillane's book *Kiss Me Deadly* was the first mystery to appear on the *New York Times* best-seller list, and during the middle of the twentieth century, Spillane could lay claim to having written seven of the top ten best-selling novels in the United States. Spillane quickly developed a reputation for writing a novel only when he needed the money (and then turning out the book within a matter of weeks, if not days), but he always provided what his readers expected: a blood-drenched crime novel in which Hammer delivers the goods. Despite some criticism (occasionally warranted, we grant you) from Gloria Steinem and her pals, Spillane's extreme version of the private-eye novel will always remain in style. Pick up *I, the Jury*, in which Hammer swears he will get revenge on the murderer of a friend, and be prepared for a violent literary thrill ride you won't forget.

NOW READ: Max Allen Collins

Max Allen Collins has always been a fan of the classic hard-boiled private eye, and he even completed for publication three manuscripts that Spillane left behind. But when he first began writing, Collins created protagonists who were in many ways antiheroic, including an aging thief and a hit man. For Collins, the problem was finding a way to bring the iconic shamus of the 1930s and 1940s into the modern world. Collins solved this literary hurdle by setting his series featuring Nathan "Nate" Heller in the past. As is Hammer, Heller is more than ready to use a gun (or a woman) when necessary, and his tough-as-nails personality will definitely remind readers of Spillane's classic detective. Collin's action-driven plots center on a number of different historical events, including the capture of John Dillinger, the assassination of Huey Long, and the mafia's first attempts to take over Las Vegas. Readers should start with *True Detective*, in which Heller is hired to protect the mayor of Chicago and find a beautiful actress's missing brother, and you'll swear you are reading a private-eye novel right out of the Golden Age.

John D. MacDonald

Long before today's crop of environmentally conscious mystery writers began their literary careers, there was John D. MacDonald and his color-coded mystery series. Although MacDonald's Travis McGee books are frequently classified as private-eye novels, McGee himself is technically not a private eye, because he carries no license. Instead, McGee refers to himself as a salvage expert, and he accepts jobs "recovering" wealth or property for deserving individuals. It isn't really a surprise that MacDonald would create an unconventional gumshoe, because he often complained of the restrictions writers faced when crafting traditional private detective stories—the limitations of the first-person voice were a particular annoyance—but McGee's cynical outlook on life and willingness to battle corruption in any form give him a free pass into the world of Spade and Marlowe. Living on a houseboat called *The Busted Flush* in Florida, McGee's views toward women are nearly Cro-Magnon by today's standards, but his concern for the environment gives the series an almost-modern flavor. Try giving readers *The Deep Blue Goodbye*, in which McGee is hired by a newly paroled prisoner who wants him to find some money—money that McGee quickly discovers belongs to someone else, who isn't exactly thrilled with the idea of giving back.

NOW READ: Randy Wayne White

Having received the John D. MacDonald Award for Literary Excellence would seem to make Randy Wayne White an obvious choice as a read-alike suggestion for MacDonald's Travis McGee books, but there are other, better reasons. As with MacDonald, White has created an atypical professional detective: Marion "Doc" Ford, a Sanibel Island marine biologist and former CIA operative, who with the help of his sidekick, Tomlinson, finds himself cleaning up after a variety of deadly crimes. Setting also plays an important role in the Ford-Tomlinson books, and White, like MacDonald, not only brilliantly evokes both the both the sunny and the darker sides of Florida but also invests his writing with a strong concern for the environment. Give readers the first in the series, *Sanibel Flats*, in which Ford discovers a body on Sanibel Island, and MacDonald readers will be hooked.

KEY AUTHORS: NEW-SCHOOL PRIVATE DETECTIVES

A classic will always remain in fashion, but that doesn't mean readers don't enjoy something new. Here are four authors who have successfully brought the old-school private eye into the modern world.

Robert B. Parker

Robert B. Parker wrote his PhD dissertation on the works of Chandler, Hammett, and MacDonald, so it really isn't surprising that his own contribution to the mystery genre is the quintessential hard-boiled private eye Spenser (one name only, please). Parker borrowed from and built on the literary allusions and subtle humor that are the key appeal of Chandler's writing, but he also added a few new twists of his own. Unlike his literary ancestors Spade, Hammer, and Marlowe, Spenser is no lone-wolf investigator. Instead he relies on both his paramour—the psychologist Susan Silverman—and his tough-guy sidekick, Hawk, to professionally and personally keep his back, and these relationships give the series an added layer of depth and richness. Start readers off with *The Godwulf Manuscript*, Spenser's first case, in which he must find a fourteenth-century manuscript that has disappeared from a university's collection.

NOW READ: Michael Kortya

With all the changes going on in detective fiction, readers might be worried about the fate of the traditional hard-boiled private-eye novel, but after reading Michael Kortya's books featuring former cop turned private detective Lincoln Perry, they can rest assured that the future of this subgenre is secure. Kortya began writing while in college, and his second work, *Tonight I Said Goodbye*, became his first published novel, as well as the first in a series. Like Parker's, Kortya's neatly nuanced writing shows the stylistic influences of Dashiell Hammett and Raymond Chandler, from the spare, yet vivid prose to the iconic protagonist who is willing to engage in the age-old battle against corruption and deceit to find the truth. Start with *Tonight I Said Goodbye*, in which Perry and his partner, Joe Pritchard, investigate the "suicide" of another Cleveland private investigator, and you are certain to be back for more.

Walter Mosley

Walter Mosley's Easy Rawlins books are not just terrific hard-boiled private detective stories; they are thoughtful and thorough social explorations of race and class in America. If Chandler delved into the corruption and crime of the white world of Los Angeles in the 1930s, Mosley takes on the difficult task of being African American in the same city beginning in the late 1940s. From missing persons to McCarthyism and union troubles, the plots of the Rawlins bleak and dark mysteries are firmly anchored in their time and place, but it is Mosley's vividly written characters—from reluctant sleuth Easy to his psychopathic sidekick, Mouse—who truly remain with the reader. Give readers the first in the series, *Devil in a Blue Dress*, in which Easy, after being fired from his factory job, agrees to find a woman in a blue dress for a shifty mobster.

NOW READ: James Sallis

James Sallis has written nonfiction and poetry, and he has even translated other writers' novels. Sallis brings all these literary experiences to his series featuring Lewis "Lew" Griffin, an African American private detective who specializes in missing-person cases, and this series makes an especially good suggestion for those readers impatiently awaiting the next Easy Rawlins mystery. In his sextet of Lew Archer books, Sallis not only gives readers a wonderfully atmospheric mix of hard-boiled style, polished literary writing, and a quintessential private detective whose cases are almost always connected to the African American experience in this country, but also delivers the same quietly powerful writing and subtle depth of characterization found in Mosley's work. Begin with Lew's first book, *The Long-Legged Fly*, in which Lew finds himself involved in four different cases over several different decades.

Robert Crais

Blame it on Chandler. After discovering Raymond Chandler's novel *The Little Sister*, Robert Crais knew he had to write his own detective novel, but Crais's path to publication took a few unexpected twists before he wrote his first mystery. Crais actually spent more than a decade writing for such hit television shows as *Hill Street Blues*, *Miami Vice*, and *Cagney and Lacey* before his first mystery, *The Monkey's Raincoat*, was published in 1987. The novel introduced readers to West Hollywood private investigator Elvis Cole, a smart, smart-mouthed detective known for his loud Hawaiian shirts, his love of cooking and classic rock, and his yellow Corvette, who takes on the job of finding a woman's missing husband and son. Elvis is aided in his investigations by his partner, Joe Pike, a former LA police officer turned mercenary who acts as Elvis' darker half, someone who isn't afraid to use force or violence to achieve a goal. Although Crais's television writing background is evident in the series's fast-paced dialogue, colorful characters, and cinematic plot twists, his literary creation Cole is in many ways the quintessential private eye, a cynic on the outside and a romantic on the inside, someone with a strong personal code of honor who battles corruption and fights for justice. This is a series that is best started at the beginning, so steer readers toward *The Monkey's Raincoat*, in which Elvis and Joe discover that a seemingly simple missing person's case is anything but simple.

NOW READ: **Bob Morris**

If you are looking for a new author to try after binging on Robert Crais, we suggest Bob Morris. Not only is it not much of a stretch to go from the sunny skies and wafting palm trees of LA to the sandy beaches of Florida, but more important, Morris has Crais's wit (titles like *Jamaica Me Dead* and *Bermuda Schwartz* give you some idea of his sense of humor) and ability to tell a fast-paced, page-turning tale, populated with equally colorful (and usually edgy) characters. In Morris's first book, *Bahamarama*, Zack Chasteen, a former football player and ex-con, is on his way to see his girlfriend when she is kidnapped and her ex-boyfriend is murdered, and guess who is suspect No. 1?

S. J. Rozan

Most mystery authors consider themselves fortunate if they are able to create one memorable sleuth. S. J. Rozan (a New York City architect by training) is doubly gifted in that she writes a private-eye series featuring two distinctive, yet equally entertaining detectives—Lydia Chin and Bill Smith—and does so with amazing skill. Beginning with *China Trade*, which is narrated in Chin's voice and concerns a missing cache of Chinese porcelain stolen from a museum, Rozan deftly alternates literary viewpoint with each book in the series. The novels told from Smith's point of view have the classic, laconic tone found in the best of Chandler's books, whereas many of Chin's cases have some connection to the Chinese culture that is an important part of New York City. A common element found in both the Chin and the Smith novels is the quality of Rozan's writing: sharp, unique, and unforgettable.

NOW READ: **Dennis Lehane**

Like Rozan, Dennis Lehane offers mystery readers a hard-boiled, urban private-eye series featuring two detectives—a man and a woman—working together to solve cases. Just as Chin and Smith depend on each other to keep the other's back during a case, so do Lehane's Patrick Kenzie and Angela Gennaro, friends and now partners in their Boston-based detective firm. Like Rozan, Lehane also adds in a strongly evoked sense of place to the series, and Lehane has a distinctive literary voice that neatly translates the classic writing style of masters of private detective fiction like Chandler into the twenty-first century. Begin with Kenzie and Gennaro's first case, *A Drink before the War*, in which the duo is hired to find a cleaning woman who disappeared with some important documents that someone is willing to kill to retrieve.

KEY AUTHORS: THE DISTAFF PRIVATE EYE

Women may have had only two choices—secretary or slut—when the private-eye subgenre began, but it wasn't long before ladies were demanding their equal place alongside Spade and Spenser. Here are three female private eyes who prove that, once and for all, being a gumshoe is not (as the title of P. D. James groundbreaking Cordelia Gray novel reminds us) an unsuitable job for a woman.

Sue Grafton

There is more to Sue Grafton's Kinsey Millhone books that just a bunch of titles cleverly connected to the alphabet; Grafton has given the PI subgenre one of its more nuanced and entertaining sleuths. Although Grafton gives a literary nod to her hard-boiled counterparts (especially by setting her books in Santa Teresa, a fictionalized version of Santa Barbara, California, a locale Ross MacDonald also uses in his Lew Archer mysteries), Grafton departs from the old school of private eyes by giving her fictional sleuth a past and then gradually sharing it with readers over the course of the series. Readers discover not only Kinsey's realistic quirks, such as the peanut butter and pickle sandwiches she loves to eat and the beat-up Volkswagen she drives, but also, and more important, her own realistically complicated personal relationships, such as the one with her ex-husband. Start readers off with *A Is for Alibi*, in which convicted murderer Niki Fife hires Kinsey to find the real killer, and the majority will find themselves planning on seeing Kinsey's adventures through until Z.

NOW READ: Laura Lippman

Laura Lippman likes to call Tess Monaghan, her fictional sleuth, an accidental private investigator, in part because it isn't until the third book in the series that Tess, an unemployed journalist willing to take any freelance job to pay the rent, actually obtains her private-eye license. But even though it may have taken Tess a few books to catch up with Kinsey, Lippman's series, which has won every major American mystery award, is still a good suggestion for fans of Grafton's mysteries. Tess is not quite the loner that Kinsey is—Tess manages to maintain her sense of independence and still stay closely connected to her family and friends—but readers who enjoy Grafton's subtle, yet sharp sense of humor will find that Lippman seasons her own writing with an equally dry sense of wit. In addition, Lippman delivers the same expertly crafted plots and captivating characters that readers have come to expect from Grafton. Start with *Baltimore Blues*—in which Tess accepts a job from a friend to follow his fiancée, only to find that the trail leads to murder—and readers are certain to want to book another visit soon to Lippman's Charm City.

Sara Paretsky

With her V. I. Warshawski books, author Sara Paretsky wanted to write more than just a generic private-eye mystery. She wanted to take on important social issues of the day and, at the same time, give the male-dominated subgenre a much-needed shot of estrogen. On all counts Paretsky succeeded not only in creating one of the genre's most popular detectives but also in delivering powerful, hard-boiled stories about corporate corruption, civil rights, and city politics. At the same time Paretsky's books, like the best of the classic private-eye novels, evoke a strong sense of place: in this case the Windy City: Chicago. First introduced in *Indemnity Only*, in which a banker hires the sleuth to find his son's missing girlfriend, Victoria Iphigenia ("Vic" to her friends) has a passion for seeing justice done that extends throughout the series. With her V. I. Warshawski mysteries, Paretsky has created a strong female sleuth who isn't afraid to go toe-to-toe with tough guys or tackle tough social issues to see that justice is served.

NOW READ: Linda Barnes

Once your readers have finished all the V. I. Warshawski books, you can successfully steer them to Linda Barnes's books featuring Carlotta Carlyle, another strong-willed, strongly opinionated female detective with a deep commitment to both people and justice. Half Irish, half Jewish, Carlotta works both as private eye and a part-time cab driver in Boston. Just as V. I. has become synonymous with the Windy City, Carlotta has become identified with Bean Town, and this strong sense of place comes through in all of Barnes's books featuring Carlotta. In addition, Barnes, like Paretsky, gives her fictional feminist sleuth plenty of hard-boiled cases involving tough social issues, including money laundering, illegal immigration, and drugs. This is another series best started at the beginning, so readers should pick up *A Trouble of Fools*, in which Carlotta is asked to find a missing Irishman who left behind an unexplained $13,000.

Marcia Muller

Before there were Kinsey and V. I., there was Sharon. Marcia Muller's first mystery featuring Sharon McCone, *Edwin of the Iron Shoes*, was published in 1978 and introduced readers to McCone, who started out her detecting career working as staff investigator for the All Souls Legal Cooperative in San Francisco. McCone was the first of the new brand of American female private detectives: women who were every bit as tough and competent as their male counterparts but who also had the same day-to-day problems and complicated personal lives of any woman in the late twentieth century. Nearly three decades later, Muller has added and dropped secondary characters in McCone's life and given her a new job and a few long-term romantic relationships, but McCone's dedication to detection remains consistent, and for McCone's fans, the series remains consistently entertaining.

NOW READ: Valerie Wilson Wesley

Much to the delight of many readers, Marcia Muller introduced one of the first nuanced, realistic female sleuths into the genre with Sharon McCone, and Valerie Wilson Wesley, a former editor-at-large for *Essence* magazine, successfully continues that trend with her character of Tamara Hayle, an African American private eye and divorced mother. As does McCone, Hayle struggles with the pressures modern society imposes on women—especially working mothers—and Hayle brings both her professional expertise and her personal compassion to each of her cases. Start readers off with the first in the series, *When Death Comes Stealing*, in which Tamara worries that her son Jamal may be next when her ex-husband asks her to investigate the death of two of his other sons from different women.

NOTES

1. Raymond Chandler, *The Simple Art of Murder* (New York: Vintage Books, 1988), 18.
2. "The Shamus Awards: Bestowed by the Private Eye Writers of America," *Thrilling Detective*, www.thrillingdetective.com/trivia/triv72.html.

6

POLICE PROCEDURALS
They Got the Beat

Perhaps it's the fascination of watching others work that makes procedural mysteries so popular. After all, who doesn't want to know the inside scoop? Need more proof? Just look at the popularity of this subgenre of mysteries in the world of television, from that 1950s classic *Dragnet* to today's never-ending permutations of *CSI* and *Law and Order*. Procedural mysteries deliver the kind of fascinating forensic details and scientific techniques that the forces of law use to solve crimes, and some mystery readers crave those. But there is more to procedurals than just microscopes and DNA. The best law enforcement agents always rely on their own intuition—a hunch—that tells them when something about a suspect's story doesn't ring true. A truly compelling procedural blends both kinds of investigative techniques into one seamless story.

The greatest procedural writers either have a background in the profession themselves or have some strong connection to law enforcement that allows them to deliver the goods. Authors with their own police experience include Dorothy Uhnak, whose years as a New York City police officer give her books that vivid sense of realism readers demand, and Joseph Wambaugh, who spent fourteen years as a detective sergeant in the Los Angeles Police Department before retiring to write both crime fiction and nonfiction. Although a personal connection to the police world can help create an authentic atmosphere for many authors, it is not a prerequisite. Ed McBain, who never worked on a police force in his life, is an excellent example, in that he created the quintessential fictional cop shop in the form of the Eighty-Seventh Precinct. Michael Connelly used the insider knowledge he gained working as a police reporter when it came time for him to create his series featuring LAPD homicide detective Hieronymus "Harry" Bosch. The ability of an author to authentically re-create the world of a professional crime solver—whether through actual experience or tons of careful research and vivid writing—is vital, because this is a major appeal factor for many procedural readers.

Most procedural mysteries focus on the world of police work, but there are several successful procedural mystery series that stretch the boundaries of the subgenre in new and interesting ways. Millions of readers have been introduced to the world of the medical examiner's office and their role in crime solving through the novels of Patricia Cornwell and Kathy Reichs. When Cornwell's first book, *Postmortem*, was published in 1990, it introduced many readers to the world of the medical examiner's office—well, at least those readers too young to remember *Quincy, M.E.*! And author Linda Fairstein brings another element to the procedural subgenre: the role of the district attorney's office in crime solving.

An important thing to remember when working with procedural readers (and actually with readers of any mystery subgenre) is that the tone of procedural mysteries can vary greatly. Although many procedurals do have a tough, gritty, and darker literary flavor, such as Ian Rankin's John Rebus books, this is not always true. For example, Georges Simeon's Maigret books are suffused with an almost subtle sense of Gallic charm. M. C. Beaton writes a charming procedural series featuring Constable Hamish Macbeth; it's set in the Scottish Highlands and is practically cozy in tone. In Rhys Bowen's series featuring Welsh policeman Evan Evans, he is every bit the equal of his big-city police counterparts when it comes to solving a murder but is not the typical hard-boiled cop.

KEY AUTHORS: OLD-SCHOOL COPS

There are scores of excellent procedurals available today, books that put readers right out there with the thin blue line fighting crime. But for our money, here are three police procedural series—let's call them the holy trinity—that no mystery reader should miss.

Ed McBain

Because Evan Hunter was brilliant in so many writing formats (including the screenplay for *The Birds*, the novel *The Blackboard Jungle*, and his memoir of working with Alfred Hitchcock), it is easy to forget his Eighty-Seventh Precinct books, which he wrote as Ed McBain. Set in an imaginary city, a thinly disguised New York, the fifty-odd books are populated by a large cast of cops, including Meyer Meyer, Bert Kling, and Steve Carella, and they are perhaps the most perfect distillation of the police procedural. Carella is the main character of most of the Precinct novels, but each cop has his day in the sun, and occasionally even a villain, like the Deaf Man, moves to center stage. What McBain brought to the procedural subgenre was the concept that when it comes to solving crimes, good police officers work in teams, and this is one of the main appeal factors of his Precinct novels. McBain's writing is as realistically dark as police work itself, but it is also tempered by humor and irony. Start with the first, *Cop Hater*, in which Detective Steve Carella must find out who is killing other detectives of the Eighty-Seventh Precinct, but don't miss *Fuzz*, in which the men of the precinct attempt to once and for all stop the brilliantly maniacal Deaf Man.

NOW READ: Archer Mayor

In theory the small town of Brattleboro, Vermont, could not be more different than the big city of New York, but the reality is that Archer Mayor's Joe Gunther series has much in common with Ed McBain's Eighty-Seventh Precinct books. Both McBain and Mayor are more interested in the process of how police work a case rather than only their solution to a crime, and this shows through in their writing. In addition, although Mayor's cast of characters might not be quite as large as McBain's, he populates his series with an equally convincing group of supporting characters, including Brattleboro chief of police Tony Brandt and fellow police officers J. P. Tyler, Sammie Martens, and Ron Klesczewski, all of whom play their parts in helping Gunther with cases. The Joe Gunther books can be read and enjoyed in any order, but readers should start with the first title, *Open Season*, in which Gunther investigates the sudden murders of several jurors who sat on a high-profile case.

Joseph Wambaugh

If your reader wants gritty realism in police procedurals, Joseph Wambaugh easily tops the list of recommended authors. The son of a policeman and a working LA police detective for fifteen years, Wambaugh brings readers right into the squad room and then lets them see what really happens in the average day of a working cop. Wambaugh's first book, *The New Centurions*, rose to No. 1 on the *New York Times* best-seller list. He followed it with other police classics: *The Blue Knight*, *The Choirboys*, and *The Black Marble*. In addition to his novels, Wambaugh wrote several true-crime books, including the best-seller *The Onion Field*, and he created the hit 1970s television series *Police Story*. Wambaugh's police novels are characterized by their convincing view of police work, the author's respect for the thin blue line that keeps society safe, black humor, and memorable characters who struggle with inner demons while trying to maintain fragile personal relationships. Any of Wambaugh's novels are good bets for procedural fans, but try starting with his first book, *The New Centurions*, which tells the story of how three new police recruits survive their first year on the force.

NOW READ: William J. Caunitz
For three decades, William J. Caunitz worked for the New York Police Department (including time spent with famed corruption buster Frank Serpico) and, like Wambaugh, Caunitz uses his own experiences on the force to invest his powerfully written procedural novels with gritty realism. From walking a beat to captaining a team of officers, Caunitz doesn't miss a detail, and his books are perfect for readers who want more of the authentic police experience in their detective fiction. Start with *One Police Plaza*, in which NYPD lieutenant Daniel Malone discovers that several different people—including some highly placed cops in the department—want him to drop his investigation into the routine murder of a young woman.

Michael Connelly

If you're looking for a little more in your police procedural, a few more layers to the characters, a little more atmosphere, and a lot more poetry in the writing style, then you're looking for Michael Connelly. Connelly got his literary start writing for newspapers, eventually becoming a crime reporter for the *Los Angeles Times*. When he burst onto the mystery scene with his first book, *The Black Echo*, featuring LAPD detective Hieronymus "Harry" Bosch, critics and readers stepped back and said, "Whoa!" They recognized that an old soul disguised as a new talent had just arrived on the mystery scene, with a riveting tale about a complicated protagonist struggling to come to terms with his past while trying to build a future for himself as a police detective. *The Black Echo* won the Edgar Award for Best First Mystery Novel, and that was just the beginning of Connelly's distinguished career, which now includes more than fourteen Bosch books, some stand-alone titles, a few Mickey Haller books, and awards too numerous to list. If McBain and Wambaugh represent the best of old-school police procedurals, Connelly's Bosch books demonstrate that the subgenre is in good hands. Start off readers new to Connelly with his first book *The Black Echo*, in which Bosch, while investigating a drug-related death at Mulholland Dam, recognizes the victim as a former soldier with whom he served in Vietnam.

NOW READ: T. Jefferson Parker

Readers who enjoy the rich, layered characterization; the deftly evoked Southern California setting; and the literary flavor of Connelly's crime novels will find that T. Jefferson Parker delivers equally satisfying stories. Parker, a critically acclaimed and award-winning former newspaper reporter, has been compared to the gods of the mystery novel, Dashiell Hammett and Raymond Chandler. His plots are complex and clever, and his characters keep readers turning the pages long past their bedtimes. Although the majority of Parker's books are stand-alone titles, he has two series, one featuring Orange County sheriff's deputy Merci Rayborn, and one series featuring Charlie Hood, an LA County deputy. If you love a good series, try the Charlie Hood books, starting with *LA Outlaws*, in which Charlie hunts down a female Robin Hood. But our favorite Parker book is his Edgar Award–winning stand-alone mystery *Silent Joe.* Joe is a classic flawed hero trying to solve his father's murder. It's a story of revenge and redemption, wrapped in Parker's usual gripping writing style.

KEY AUTHORS: THE UNIQUE POLICE BEAT

For decades, it seemed that if you wanted to write a police procedural series, you had two choices for your setting: New York City or Los Angeles. However, the following authors prove that a good cop can be found anywhere there are crimes needing to be solved.

Tony Hillerman

Tony Hillerman's books are lessons on Native American culture disguised as riveting police procedural mysteries. This is exactly why so many readers love his books: both for the compelling, carefully crafted plots and for the insight they provide into a different world. It isn't surprising that Hillerman would eventually choose to write about Native Americans; his own background includes a strong connection to the Native American culture, as he was raised with Native Americans, went to an Indian boarding school, and generally lived among his own characters for much of his life. During World War II, Hillerman returned home after being injured in combat, and while driving a truck out to the Navajo reservation, he saw a curing ceremony called the Enemy Way. The experience inspired him to begin his first mystery, *The Blessing Way*, which introduced readers to Navajo Tribal Police Detective Joe Leaphorn, but it was not until the fourth book in the series, *The Listening Woman*, that Hillerman's other main detective, Tribal Police Officer Jim Chee, became part of the cast of characters. Leaphorn and Chee represent the sometimes-conflicting aspects of Native American life: the attempt to blend into the modern world and the ongoing wish to retain their own past. In addition, an underlying theme of all but one of Hillerman's books is the clash both between Navajo culture and the rest of the world and between traditional tribal police and outside police departments. Not only are Hillerman's books great mysteries; they have introduced millions of readers to the fascinating world of the Navajo people. Begin with *The Blessing Way*, in which Leaphorn begins to wonder whether supernatural forces might be involved when a corpse turns up with a mouthful of sand, and you will find yourself setting out on an unforgettable journey into another culture.

NOW READ: P. L. Gaus

What many readers love most about Hillerman's books is how they introduce them to a fascinating and different culture in the context of a mystery novel. Readers will find that they have the same illuminating experience with the works of P. L. Gaus, set in the Amish country of Ohio. Gaus writes with great knowledge and tremendous regard for the Amish people, and his mysteries feature the sleuths Professor Michael Branden, Pastor Caleb Troyer, and Sheriff Bruce Robertson, who work together to keep the peace in their community. In addition, the clash between old Native American traditions and the modern world in Hillerman's mysteries is echoed in Gaus's books in the sometimes-conflicting values of the Amish and the modern world. Begin readers with the first book, *Blood of the Prodigal*, in which Branden, Troyer, and Robertson first team up to solve a kidnapping and murder in the Amish community.

Georges Simenon

For more than forty years and across seventy-six novels, Georges Simenon wrote about the adventures of Inspector Jules Maigret of the Police Judiciaire, a police officer who relies more on his ability to understand human nature than on forensic science to solve crimes. Dedicated in equal measures to his marriage and his next meal, Maigret might seem to be the quintessential Frenchman, but he is equally committed to his job. It is Maigret's ability to unobtrusively insert himself into the scene of a murder that allows him to absorb every detail he needs to later solve the crime before he quietly returns home to his beloved Madame Maigret and whatever dish she has prepared for his dinner. Although it is not necessary to read the Maigret series in order (and they were not written in strict chronological order, either, or even published in English in order), give readers *Maigret and the Enigmatic Lett*, in which Maigret must determine exactly who the mysterious Lett was, for a soupçon of Simenon's Gallic-flavored brand of police procedural.

NOW READ: Magdalen Nabb

What France is to Simenon's Maigret books, so is Italy to the Salvatore Guarnaccia mysteries of Magdalen Nabb. English by birth, Nabb moved to Italy and quickly fell in love with the country, so much so that she chose to set her mysteries in her new homeland. Nabb enriches all of her novels with a vivid sense of life in Florence and the surrounding Tuscan countryside—both that which the typical tourist encounters and the day-to-day details known only to longtime residents. Like his creator, Carabinieri Marshal Guarnaccia is not a native of Florence; he is a Sicilian police officer posted to the northern Italian city, where he must quickly learn to adapt. Guarnaccia shares a similar, almost leisurely approach to police work with Maigret, using his intuitive skills and his understanding of human nature to bring his cases to a successful conclusion. Begin with *Death of an Englishman*, in which Guarnaccia investigates when an Englishman is found dead in an antiques-filled apartment.

James Lee Burke

James Lee Burke began his career as a "serious" writer, but after his second and third novels failed to achieve the critical success of his first book, Burke nearly gave up writing forever. While struggling to publish his fourth novel, Burke took the advice of a friend and wrote a mystery, *The Neon Rain*, which not only initiated a bidding war among publishers but also became the first in Burke's long-running Dave Robicheaux series. At the beginning of the series, Robicheaux is a New Orleans police detective, but by the end of the first book, he has left the force to open up a bait and boat shop in the bayou country of New Iberia. Robicheaux does a bit of freelance investigating, but he soon is back on the job as a detective for New Iberia's Sheriff Department. For mystery readers the Robicheaux books are an irresistible combination of a complex, complicated protagonist (Robicheaux not only battles alcoholism but also has long struggled with depression and post-traumatic stress disorder from his service in the Vietnam War) but also dark, thoughtful plots written with an elegant, poetic sense of style. Burke strongly believes that setting is a major influence on both characters and plot, so it isn't surprising that the Robicheaux books are rich with the flavor of New Orleans and the bayou country, which contributes yet another layer of appeal to this compelling series. If you are ready to take a trip to Cajun country, start with *The Neon Rain*, in which Robicheaux's investigation into the murder of a prostitute found in the bayou costs him his badge and nearly his life.

NOW READ: Sharyn McCrumb

McCrumb got her mystery career started with an amateur sleuth series featuring Elizabeth MacPherson and two detective novels that cleverly spoofed the fantasy and science-fiction genres, but she is best known for her Ballad books, a series of mysteries based on American folklore and set in the Appalachian Mountains. In these eloquently written books, all of which have a strong sense of place, McCrumb blurs the boundaries between mystery fiction and literature, which makes the books an excellent suggestion for fans of James Lee Burke's lyrical Robicheaux books. Start with the first title in the series, *If Ever I Return, Pretty Peggy-O*, in which Sheriff Spencer Arrowood investigates the threats against Peggy Muryan, a once-popular folksinger who has just moved back to her small Tennessee hometown.

James Church

The last place on earth most people would imagine as a setting for a procedural series is North Korea, a country whose repressive government has created an iron curtain of secrecy about its people and culture. Yet this is exactly the place James Church, the pseudonym for a former Western intelligence officer, has chosen for his series featuring Inspector O, a state security officer who struggles to maintain the delicate balance between his professional integrity and the realities of working and living in a dangerous police state. With the Inspector O series, Church wanted not only to give readers a compelling detective dedicated to solving crimes but also to introduce readers to the fascinating country of North Korea and give them an accurate and honest view of a place about which many of us know nothing. Church succeeds brilliantly on both counts. Start with the first book in the series, *A Corpse in Koryo*, in which Inspector O investigates the murder of a foreigner in the capital city.

NOW READ: Rebecca Pawel

Rebecca Pawel's award-winning series featuring Sergeant Tejada Alonzo y Leon of the Guardia Civil is set decades before Church's Inspector O books, there are several similar appeal elements that make this a good read-alike choice. Not only must Tejada try to solve murders while living under a similarly restrictive (and often dangerous) political regime, but also there is the same strong sense of time and place found in Church's books, as Pawel brilliantly re-creates the mood and atmosphere of post–Civil War Spain with fascinating detail about what life was like for those living under Francisco Franco's rule. Begin readers with the first book in the series, *Death of a Nationalist*, in which Tejada finds his investigation into the murder of a comrade becoming entangled with the fate of a wounded Republican in hiding.

KEY AUTHORS: "CIVILIZED" COPS

When most readers hear "police procedural," they immediately think of cynical, tough big-city cops whose investigations take them into the darkest corners of society. But long before Joseph Wambaugh and Ed McBain were writing about cops and crimes, British authors such as Ngaio Marsh and Josephine Tey were crafting mysteries featuring the inspectors and chief inspectors of Scotland Yard. These Golden Age police procedurals were quite different in tone, though, from their later American counterparts, in that they focused less on a gritty, realistic take on police work and instead more on a traditional, classically structured mystery. Although some might think aristocratic cops went out of style with tea cozies and antimacassars, the more civilized variation of the police detective continues to thrive today in mysteries.

P. D. James

P. D. (Phyllis Dorothy) James has written several stand-alone novels and two series, but her books featuring Scotland Yard commander Adam Dagliesh are an excellent modern update of the civilized branch of the police procedural subgenre. A former British civil servant, James turned to writing as a means of supplementing her family's income, but her books became so popular that James soon retired and dedicated herself to a life of crime writing. James's writing is elegant, there is always a strong sense of place in her books, and her focus is frequently on characterization rather than forensic science as a key to solving the crime. With her subtly nuanced characterization, literary approach to detective writing, and gift for crafting clever plots, it is no wonder that millions of readers love James and know her as the new Queen of Crime. Some readers will want to start the Dagliesh series with the first book, *Cover Her Face*, in which the detective is called in to find the killer of a beautiful housemaid from among a houseful of suspects, but you might want to give readers one of James's later books, such as *A Taste for Death*, in which the bodies of both a politician and a homeless man are found together in a church, so they can get a good taste of her subtle characterization and sumptuous prose.

NOW READ: Colin Dexter

Just as James's elegantly written Dagliesh books are the perfect synthesis of the traditional puzzle-based Golden Age mystery and today's more literary-flavored crime novel, so, too, are Colin Dexter's Chief Inspector Morse mysteries. Like James, Dexter understands and values the roots of the mystery genre, and all of his Morse books deliver a solidly constructed, fiendishly clever mystery. Dexter also writes with the same literary flair and nuanced characterization found in James's work, and his mysteries, like hers, gently steer the crime novel into the realm of literature. The best introduction to Dexter's work is Morse's first case (with his long-suffering assistant, Sergeant Lewis), *The Last Bus to Woodstock*, in which Morse investigates the murder of a secretary who was last seen hitchhiking on a road near Oxford.

Elizabeth George

American author Elizabeth George is another writer of the urbane brand of police procedural with her series featuring New Scotland Yard's Inspector Thomas Lynley and Police Sergeant Barbara Havers. George's books are stylishly written with a remarkable depth of characterization—there is often as much focus on the two detectives' private lives as on the actual investigation itself—and complicated plots that unfold at a leisurely (some might say glacial) pace. Working-class Havers provides a welcome contrast to the aristocratic, wealthy Lynley when they are first introduced and forced to work together in *A Great Deliverance*, but their adversarial professional relationship turns into an unexpected friendship as the series develops. One readers' advisory caveat to keep in mind with George's books: because the tangled personal relationships between her cast of characters extend over the series and events in one book can have repercussions in another, George's Lynley and Havers books are best read in order, so readers should start off with *A Great Deliverance*, in which Lynley and Havers are sent to the wilds of Yorkshire to investigate what seems to be an easily solvable murder, only to find themselves involved in a confusingly complex case.

NOW READ: Deborah Crombie

Initially, the common denominator in Elizabeth George's and Deborah Crombie's mysteries would seem to be the authors themselves: both are American women writing police procedurals set in Great Britain that feature the pairing of an aristocratic sleuth with another detective who is not quite of his class. But there are other elements that make Crombie's books a good read-alike choice for fans of George's novels. Crombie's series featuring Duncan Kincaid and Gemma James are as much about the characters and how their personal lives can affect an investigation as about the traditionally constructed plot itself. As the Kincaid and James series has progressed, Crombie's writing has become richer and more layered, thus making the connection to George's books even stronger. Although it is not the first in the series, start readers with the elegantly written, richly nuanced *Dreaming of the Bones*, in which Kincaid investigates the "suicide" of a poet for his ex-wife, Victoria, despite the effect it will have on his new relationship with James.

Louise Penny

Former radio journalist and broadcaster Louise Penny is new to the mystery world, but her award-winning series featuring Chief Inspector Armand Gamache of the Sûreté du Québec is an excellent example of how the classic British style of police procedurals can still work with readers today. Nuanced characterization, a leisurely civilized pace, and vividly detailed settings are the key elements in all of her Armand Gamache books, which is the reason the series has garnered not only numerous awards but also a growing readership. As with other contemporary procedural series, teamwork plays an important part in Penny's books, and Gamache relies on the other members of his group to help him solve the case at hand. But in some ways Gamache is also a reflection of the older, Maigret school of police work through his thoughtful questions and his gift for intuition rather than depending just on the science of forensics to solve murders. Readers new to Penny will want to start at the beginning with *Still Life*, in which Gamache tries to find out who would want to kill an elderly artist in the small Canadian village of Three Pines.

NOW READ: Donna Leon

Readers who have enjoyed Louise Penny's modern take on the classic police procedural mystery will definitely want to try Donna Leon's books featuring Commissario Guido Brunetti of the Venice police. Leon's Brunetti novels unfold in the same relaxed manner as Penny's books, Leon's attention to setting is every bit the equal of Penny's, and Brunetti's style of police detection shares many similar characteristics with Gamache's thoughtful, character-driven approach to solving crimes. *Murder at La Fenice*, in which a much-hated conductor is murdered during an intermission of *La Traviata*, is an excellent introduction to Leon's civilized brand of police procedurals.

KEY AUTHORS: THE NON-COP PROCEDURAL

Although the type of detective most commonly connected to the procedural subgenre is a cop, the truth is that any professional involve in crime solving can serve as a winning fictional sleuth, as the following authors capably demonstrate.

Patricia Cornwell

With her first book *Postmortem*, which won every major mystery award on both sides of the Atlantic when it was published in 1990, author Patricia Cornwell proved that a successful procedural mystery is not always about cops. What readers do expect is that the author deliver a vividly detailed account of how some professional—such as a forensics expert—plays an important role in solving crimes. Before writing *Postmortem*—which introduces readers to Doctor Kay Scarpetta, the chief medical examiner for the commonwealth of Virginia—Cornwell, a former crime journalist, first volunteered at the Richmond Medical Examiner's office and then landed a job there as a technical writer and computer analyst. The time Cornwell spent working at the examiner's office—and attending autopsies—was time well spent, as it gives her Kay Scarpetta books a graphic yet realistically convincing literary flavor. With the occasional help of police officer Peter Marino, Scarpetta has gone on to solve a number of puzzling—and usually gruesomely detailed—murders while providing mystery readers with a front-row seat at the morgue. If you are ready to start reading Cornwell, lock your doors and pick up *Postmortem*, in which Scarpetta tangles with a psychopathic murderer.

NOW READ: Karin Slaughter

Karin Slaughter might not have the same prior professional experience that Patricia Cornwell and Kathy Reichs bring to their procedurals, but Slaughter has done her homework when it comes to detective work. Slaughter's gritty and graphic mysteries, and in particular her Grant County series—featuring doctor and coroner Sarah Linton; her ex-husband, the chief of police Jeffrey Tolliver; and the detective Lena Adams—delivers the same realistic thrills and chills that readers expect from Cornwell and Reichs. Readers will also find that, like Cornwell's Scarpetta, Slaughter's characters bring quite a bit of personal baggage along with them as they attempt to solve their latest case. Begin with the first in the series, *Blindsighted*, in which Sara, Jeffrey, and Lena must find a way to work together while investigating the grisly murders of several young women.

Kathy Reichs

Kathy Reichs's own life seems at times to be the real-life counterpart to that of her fictional detective, Temperance "Tempe" Brennan. A professor of anthropology, Reichs received her PhD from Northwestern University and is one of eighty-two forensic anthropologists certified by the American Board of Forensic Anthropology. In the real world, Reichs has used her academic knowledge to help identify decomposed bodies too badly damaged for the normal autopsy process, much in the same way that Tempe, a fortysomething forensic anthropologist, uses her skills to track down fictional killers. Reichs uses her own extensive knowledge of forensic science and experience in the field to give readers a thrilling, detailed look at the process of forensic detective work. The fascinating world of forensics detailed in Reichs's Tempe books has proved so popular that it has led to the creation of the television show *Bones* starring the same character. Start readers with *Deja Dead*, in which Tempe leaves behind a marriage on the rocks in North Carolina for a change of scenery in Quebec only to stumble across a dismembered female corpse stashed in trash bags.

NOW READ: Jefferson Bass

Much in the same way that Kathy Reichs's own academic and workplace experiences inspired her when it came time to write her first novel, so it happened for Jefferson Bass, the pseudonym for the literary partnership of Bill Blass and Jon Jefferson. The duo's first book was actually a nonfiction work called *Death's Acre*, the story of the Body Farm, a forensic research facility that Bill Blass founded and directs. When it came time to write their first novel, the two authors came up with their series sleuth Dr. Bill Brockton, a forensic anthropologist who runs an institution that performs research on dead bodies called the Body Farm (sound familiar, anyone?). Just as Reichs uses her own extensive forensic knowledge to invest her Temperance Brennan books with a vivid sense of reality, so do Blass and Jefferson, which makes their Dr. Bill Brockton books equally fascinating and compelling. Begin with *Carved in Bone*, the first in the series, in which a local county sheriff calls Brockton in for help in identifying the mummified body of a woman.

Linda Fairstein

Linda Fairstein is another author whose own work experiences—twenty-five years with the New York City District Attorney's Office—proved quite useful when it came time to create her Alex Cooper mystery series. With each book in the series, Fairstein explains how the criminal justice system works, how the attorney's office cooperates with other departments on a case, and how victims are treated and recover. In addition to providing readers with an entertaining, nail-biting mystery, each of Fairstein's Cooper books offer a vivid glimpse of one of New York's architectural or historical treasures, such as the Gracie Mansion or the Metropolitan Opera House. Begin readers with the first in the series, *Final Jeopardy*, in which Assistant District Attorney Alexandra Cooper doesn't believe that a friend who is murdered while staying at Alex's house in Martha's Vineyard was really the intended victim.

NOW READ: Edna Buchanan

For nearly two decades Edna Buchanan worked as crime reporter in Florida, earning a Pulitzer Prize for her efforts and a national audience.

Buchanan wrote several nonfiction works, including the best-selling *The Corpse Had a Familiar Face*, but she always wanted to try writing fiction. After delivering the Edgar-nominated *Nobody Lives Forever*, Buchanan settled into writing a Miami-based series featuring journalist Britt Montero. Just as Fairstein's sleuth Alex Cooper finds her job involving her in crime investigations, so does Buchanan's Montero, with both series effectively demonstrating how nonpolice professionals can play an important role in an investigation. Buchanan's Montero novels share a similar strong sense of place with Fairstein's books—although in Buchanan's case it is colorful, steamy southern Florida. And Buchanan is equally concerned with writing about the effect crime can have on its victims and their families. Begin readers with *Contents under Pressure*, in which Montero investigates when a popular African American football star dies in a car chase with the police.

7

HISTORICAL SLEUTHS
Crime through Time

There are a number of different reasons for the current popularity of the historical mystery subgenre with writers and readers. Many mystery readers simply enjoy reading about a different time and place, and historical mysteries provide the perfect ticket to the past, along with the added benefit of a good puzzle. Other readers enjoy historical mysteries because these detective stories place the reader on an equal footing with the sleuth. With the current advances in forensic technology, quite often in today's world, the identity of a murderer can be found simply by testing a bloodstain. One advantage of setting a mystery in the past is that it puts the focus of solving the crime back on to the individual sleuths, who rather than using a test tube or microscope must use their wits and reasoning skills to find the killer.

The past can also provide a whole different source of motives for crimes, motives that might not pack the same emotional punch if used in the present day. Even as recent as the 1940s, a pregnancy out of wedlock was enough to socially ruin a woman, and this might have been enough motive for that same lady to kill to keep this fact a secret. Although we might think politics and religion are hot-button topics today—topics that can easily push people into acrimonious arguments—they're nothing compared to the power these two forces had over the lives of people during the Middle Ages. During those turbulent times, believing in the "wrong" faith or backing the "wrong" ruler could very easily be cause for murder.

Writers are drawn to historical mysteries for several reasons. Some authors choose to write historical mysteries because of their expertise in a particular time period. Edward Marston uses his academic background in Elizabethan history and theater as the inspiration for his Nicholas

Bracewell series. Lynda Robinson's own anthropological knowledge of ancient Egypt inspired her to create her Lord Meren mysteries. Jacqueline Winspear was so moved by her own relatives' poignant stories about life during and after the Great War that they eventually led her to write an eloquent mystery series featuring Maisie Dobbs, whose experiences as a nurse during World War I later play a significant role in several of the cases she takes on as a private eye. These are just a few examples of authors who use their own personal and academic knowledge to create vividly detailed historical mysteries.

Writing a historical mystery also allows authors to use real historical figures as characters (and even detectives!) in their stories. Peter Lovesey uses Prince Albert of Wales as a sleuth in his Edwardian historical mystery series. Author George Baxt uses a number of Hollywood stars—including Bette Davis, Humphrey Bogart, and Greta Garbo—as detectives, whereas Ron Goulart gives Groucho Marx a secondary career as an amateur sleuth. Not only does Stephanie Barron draft Jane Austen as her literary sleuth, but also her own writing exudes a cool ironic Austenesque quality. Recently, Nicola Upson "borrowed" real-life mystery writer Josephine Tey as one part of the detecting duo in her stylish new series. These are just a few examples of writers who have chosen not only to set their mysteries in the past but also to give readers an added bonus with a "star" historical sleuth.

Historical mystery writers do walk a fine line when it comes to exactly how much historical detail to include in their stories. Fans of this subgenre want to experience life in the past, but if writers drench their plot in extraneous period details at the expense of a well-constructed mystery plot, readers will rebel. The best historical mysteries remember this and deliver a strong sense of time and place along with a clever plot.

Defining exactly what constitutes a historical mystery isn't always easy. The Crime Writers' Association of Great Britain, which has recently added an award for historical mysteries to its Dagger list, sets the cutoff date as thirty-five years before the present date. This would appear to be a concrete, easy-to-remember division, but it is by no means the only defining point for historical mysteries. For example, readers who have lived through World War II themselves might not consider a detective story set in the 1930s or 1940s as a historical mystery simply because they remember the era. So to some extent, what constitutes a historical mystery can depend in part on readers themselves.

Then there is the matter of period mysteries, those set during the author's lifetime, but now, simply because of the amount of time that has passed between the book's publication and the present day, considered a historical mystery. Both Sir Arthur Conan Doyle's Sherlock Holmes mysteries and Dorothy L. Sayers's Lord Peter Wimsey detective novels are excellent examples of this. Technically, these books are period mysteries, but historical mystery fans today might enjoy them and many other Golden Age mysteries. One important point to remember when working with period mysteries is that they reflect the time in which they were written, and this can include the author's choice of language (and slang terms) as well as views toward different ethnicities and even genders that might be a bit jarring to contemporary readers.

When it comes to historical mysteries, some readers may wish to stick to one particular era, whereas others will read any detective story set in the past. This is definitely something to discuss during the readers' advisory interview. Another caveat with this subgenre is that simply matching up mysteries by time period does not necessarily guarantee grateful acceptance by an individual reader. For example, there are a number of different writers who have produced historical mysteries set in the Victorian era, including Elizabeth Peters, Anne Perry, and Robin Paige, but each of these authors' writing styles and the tone of their series are very different.

KEY AUTHORS: BRINGING THE PAST TO LIFE

With so many excellent historical mystery writers, where do readers start? Here are four authors with a definite flair for bringing the past to life.

Ellis Peters

When it comes to awarding the title of godmother of the historical mystery subgenre, we think Ellis Peters deserves the honor. Although there were other writers turning out historical mysteries long before Peters's Brother Cadfael arrived on the scene, Peters was the first to truly popularize this subgenre with readers. Peters wrote a number of novels, historical fiction works, and a contemporary mystery series featuring Inspector George Felse before her first Brother Cadfael mystery, *A Morbid Taste for Bones*, was published in the United States in 1977, but after completing a few more contemporary Felse mysteries, Peters dedicated the rest of her literary career to creating clever puzzles for the sleuthing Benedictine monk. Inspired by different events and aspects of medieval history, including the ongoing political battle between King Stephen and Empress Maud for control of England, Peters eventually wrote twenty different adventures for Cadfael, a former soldier who turns to the church later in life. Each of the books effortlessly evokes both the glamour and the grime of twelfth-century England for readers today. Start readers off with *A Morbid Taste for Bones*, in which Cadfael, while traveling with a group of Benedictine monks to Wales to acquire the bones of a little-known saint, encounters his first murder.

NOW READ: P. C. Doherty

Writing under his own name and several different pseudonyms, P. C. Doherty is the author of ten different historical mystery series (in addition to stand-alone mysteries and several nonfiction works) set everywhere from ancient Macedonia to fifteenth-century Canterbury. Doherty's academic credentials give his mysteries the same strong sense of time and place found in Ellis Peters's Cadfael books, and his series featuring Hugh Corbett, a Chancery clerk who ends up becoming a spy for Edward I, are an especially good next read for Cadfael fans. *Satan in St. Mary's*, the first Corbett book, in which the sleuth must determine whether a recent suicide is connected to a group of Satan worshipers trying to overthrow Edward, is an excellent introduction to Doherty's concisely plotted brand of historical mysteries

Fiona Buckley

It isn't really surprising that Fiona Buckley would write such impeccably detailed historical mysteries; Fiona Buckley is the pseudonym for historical fiction author Valerie Anand. Buckley's mysteries featuring Ursula Blanchard are set during the tumultuous reign of Queen Elizabeth I, and the deadly politics of the era become an important factor in the series, beginning with the first book, *To Shield the Queen*. As the book begins, Ursula, a lady-in-waiting to Elizabeth, is given the delicate task of protecting Amy Robsart, the wife of Elizabeth's rumored romantic interest Robert Dudley. But when Amy dies in a mysterious "accident," Ursula must find out exactly what happened to clear the queen's name. Not only does Buckley give readers a plausible explanation for the real-life mystery of Amy Robsart's death, but as the series continues, Buckley effectively uses a number of fascinating real historical events of the era in her stories as Ursula finds herself not only solving mysteries but also becoming caught up in the deadly rivalry between Elizabeth and her ill-fated cousin, Mary, Queen of Scots.

NOW READ: C. J. Sansom

Readers who relish the rich sense of history and the deft use of historical figures in Buckley's Ursula Blanchard books will definitely want to give C. J. Sansom's series featuring hunchbacked lawyer Matthew Shardlake a try. Set during the tumultuous reign of Henry VIII, Sansom's darkly compelling books provide a vivid idea of just how dangerous life could be during the English Reformation as Shardlake tries to balance the demands of his own commitment to religious reform with the brutal political realities of Henry's court. Start with the first in the series, *Dissolution*, in which Matthew's boss Thomas Cromwell dispatches him to investigate when one of the king's commissioners is found beheaded at a Benedictine monastery.

Sharan Newman

Readers captivated by the combination of a vividly detailed medieval setting and a puzzling plot will want to try *Death Comes as Epiphany*, the first in Sharan Newman's well-crafted series set in twelfth-century France. Newman's books feature sleuth Catherine LeVendeur, a French novice at the beginning of the series, who is given the task by her mother superior—who just happens to be the famous Heloise (no, not she of the household hints but the medieval abbess of the French Convent of the Paraclete)—of finding out who is trying to destroy the convent's reputation. In the first book, Catherine meets Edgar of Wedderlie, and the two eventually marry. Newman excels at realistically integrating historical figures such as Heloise and Peter Abelard into a plot, and she takes great care in recreating not just the customs and costumes of the time but also the era's attitudes and beliefs. Begin with *Death Comes as Epiphany*, in which Abbess Heloise sends Catherine on a mission to the Abbey of St. Denis to discover who is trying to discredit Heloise.

NOW READ: Sharon Kay Penman

Before turning to the mystery genre, Sharon Kay Penman wrote a number of critically acclaimed historical novels, and she brings the same literary gift for evoking the past to her series featuring Justin de Quincy. Penman deftly seasons her well-plotted mysteries with colorful historical details of life in twelfth-century England, and she uses real historical figures, such as Eleanor of Aquitaine, as characters in her novels, much in the same manner that Sharan Newman does with her Catherine LeVendeur books. So, when your readers have finished everything by Sharan Newman, give them the "other" Sharon (Kay Penman, that is) beginning with *The Queen's*

Man, in which Justin finds himself caught up in a deadly mix of politics and murder after he agrees to deliver a letter for Queen Eleanor.

Margaret Frazer

Archaeologist and historian Gail Frazer began writing the Dame Frevisse medieval mysteries with her then writing partner Mary Pulver Kuhfeld as Margaret Frazer, and she continued with the Benedictine nun's adventures in sleuthing when Kuhfeld left after the sixth book. The books' colorfully detailed fifteenth-century English setting, intriguing characters, and history-rich plots give the Dame Frevisse books their vivid, you-are-really-there feeling, beginning with the first book in the series, *The Novice's Tale*, in which Frevisse investigates when the overbearing Lady Ermentrude arrives at St. Frideswide but soon winds up dead. With the Dame Frevisse books, Frazer, who also writes another series set during the reign of Henry VI featuring a traveling troop of actors, excels at re-creating the religion-centered world of the Middle Ages in the form of the Priory of St. Frideswide. Even though Frevisse may find herself entangled in the secular business of murder on a regular basis, the daily round of prayers that this no-nonsense nun follows with her Benedictine sisters keeps this sacred sleuth spiritually grounded.

NOW READ: Candace Robb

Robb's series featuring Owen Archer and Lucie Walton is a terrific next-read choice for those who have enjoyed Frazier's Dame Frevisse books. Set in fourteenth-century England, Robb's protagonist, Owen Archer, retired from service as captain of the king's archers after losing an eye in battle. Now Owen serves the lord chancellor and archbishop of York. With this series, Robb excels not only at re-creating the vibrant world of Medieval England but also at deftly blending historical fiction and classic mystery elements into one compelling story. Begin with *Apothecary Rose*, in which Owen first meets Lucie Walton, a widower and apothecary, while investigating the mysterious death of one of the archbishop's wards, who dies after drinking a potion Lucie's husband made.

KEY AUTHORS: TAKING HISTORY SERIOUSLY

Some historical mystery writers both effectively use the past as a setting for their stories and explore important concerns of the time in the framework of a mystery. Here are four good examples of authors who are unri-valed at incorporating social issues of the past into a puzzling plot.

Anne Perry

For many readers today, Anne Perry is the queen of the historical mystery subgenre. In addition to a quintet of novels set during World War I, a few set in Revolutionary France, and what some might say is a misguided attempt at writing fantasy, Perry currently writes two different histori-cal mystery series—one featuring Charlotte and Thomas Pitt and the other featuring William Monk—set during the reign of Queen Victoria. Charlotte and Thomas meet when the London police inspector investi-gates the murder of a servant in Charlotte's household in *The Cater Street Hangman*, and throughout the books, Perry lets each character play to his or her investigative strengths. In the Monk series, the protagonist is London police detective William Monk, who is suffering from amnesia after an accident. Together with Hester Latterly, a nurse who served in the Crimean War, Monk solves a number of puzzling crimes, beginning with *The Face of a Stranger*, while struggling to recall his own past history. The difference in classes and the many societal changes—such as the European grab for territory in Africa, women's suffrage, and Darwinism and evolu-tion—that are part of the Victorian era provide plenty of inspiring mate-rial for Perry's carefully constructed and often dark mysteries, which are perfect for readers who take their history seriously.

NOW READ: Deanna Raybourn

Those readers who not only relish Perry's impeccable re-creating of the Victorian era in her mysteries but also enjoy mysteries featuring husband-and-wife sleuthing teams will definitely want to add Deanna Raybourn's series featuring Lady Julia Grey and Nicholas Brisbane to their must-read lists. Readers will also find echoes of Perry's pairing of upper-class Charlotte with lower-class Thomas Pitt in Raybourn's sleuthing pair of aristocratic widow Julia and private investigator Nicholas, and, as the series progresses, their relationship, like the Pitts', turns into something much more romantically permanent. This is a series best read in order, so begin with *Silent in the Grave*, in which Julia meets Nicholas for the first time after she discovers that her late husband Edward hired him to find out who had been sending him threatening letters.

Miriam Grace Monfredo

Perry is not the only writer who manages to successfully integrate important issues of another era into a credible historical plot. Beginning with her first book, *Seneca Falls Inheritance*, Miriam Grace Monfredo uses the American past as a fascinating source of literary inspiration for her history-rich mysteries and introduces readers to librarian turned sleuth Glynis Tryon, who tries to juggle organizing the first American women's rights convention and finding a clever killer. Tryon goes on to solve further mysteries, each of which is connected to some hot-button issue of the times, such as counterfeiting, the abolitionist movement, and the Underground Railroad. As the brewing war between the North and the South eventually becomes a reality, Monfredo sends Tryon into a well-deserved retirement and then continues the series by turning the role of detective over to Tryon's younger relatives. Start with *Seneca Falls Inheritance*, in which murder interrupts Glynis's work helping Elizabeth Cady Stanton gather names of women who would support a meeting on women's rights in Seneca Falls, New York.

NOW READ: Barbara Hambly

In addition to writing one of the best genre-blurred mysteries ever—*Those Who Hunt the Night*—award-winning science fiction and fantasy writer Barbara Hambly is the author of two historical mystery series: one set in the antebellum South featuring Benjamin January and a new series written as Barbara Hamilton featuring Abigail Adams. Just as Monfredo effectively uses many of the fascinating historical conflicts of the mid-nineteenth century as grist for her literary mill, so does Hamilton with prerevolutionary America. From the dangerous politicking of the Sons of Liberty (and the role of her husband, John, in that group) to the everyday details of running a household in colonial America, Hamilton adeptly integrates them into her cleverly crafted plots, which provide the perfect mix of history and mystery. Begin with *The Ninth Daughter*, in which Abigail discovers the dead body of another woman when she pays a visit to her friend Rebecca Malvern.

Laura Joh Rowland

Laura Joh Rowland is another not-to-be-missed historical mystery writer, and her series featuring samurai Sano Ichiro and his cosleuth (and eventual partner in marriage) Lady Ueda Reiko brilliantly brings the colorful customs and class-bound culture of seventeenth-century Japan to life. Just as Perry deals with the grittier side of Victorian England, Rowland doesn't ignore the very different and sometimes quite-brutal aspects of life in Japan at that time. The series begins with *Shinju*, in which Sano believes that the ritual double suicide—or *shinju*—of beautiful, wealthy Yukiko and artist Noriyoshi is really murder and risks both his career and his life to investigate.

NOW READ: Steven Saylor

The time period and geographic setting of Steven Saylor's series featuring Gordianus the Finder could not be more different from those of Rowland's books, yet in many ways Saylor's books are a good read-alike choice for Rowland's readers. Saylor is skilled at evoking the intriguing mix of civilization and corruption found in ancient Roman society, as Rowland does with seventeenth-century Japan, and his books feature the same combination of solid historical fact and entertaining mystery fiction. Just as Rowland's Sano Ichiro frequently finds his wife "helping" him with an investigation, Saylor's Gordianus also shares sleuthing duties on occasion not only with his wife but also with other members of his family, such as his son-in-law Davus. Begin with *Roman Blood*, in which famed lawyer Cicero, whose client has been accused of murdering his father, hires Gordianus to help him with the case.

Jacqueline Winspear

With her debut novel, *Maisie Dobbs*, Jacqueline Winspear created an unforgettable heroine and started off her new series in England during the fascinating period of the 1920s and 1930s, when the specter of the Great War constantly loomed over daily life in Europe. Maisie Dobbs, once a young "tweenie" maid, eventually attends Cambridge with the help of her former employer, Lady Compton. Maisie's education is interrupted when she signs up to serve as a nurse in the "war to end all wars," and when she returns home, Maisie decides to become a private investigator. Initially, Maisie's cases might seem straightforward, but Winspear cleverly introduces enough twists and turns in each story—along with subplots that usually have some connection to World War I—to capture the reader's imagination and show how a war can still influence lives years after it is officially over. Give readers *Maisie Dobbs*, in which Maisie's first case has her trailing a wandering wife, and those same readers are certain to thank you for introducing them to a terrific new series.

NOW READ: Charles Todd

Like Winspeare, Charles Todd (a pseudonym for the mother-and-son writing team of Caroline and Charles Todd) sets the Inspector Ian Rutledge series in Great Britain after World War I, and Todd deftly explores the effect of the war on those who return home from battle as well as those left behind. Todd's series detective is Inspector Ian Rutledge, a police officer who returns to Scotland Yard after serving in France, but Rutledge is haunted by the voice of his corporal, Hamish MacLeod, whom he ordered to be executed for failing to carry out an order in combat. MacLeod in many ways acts as Rutledge's partner, and his reactions to those involved in Rutledge's cases help the inspector discover the truth. This series is best read in order, so start with the first book, *A Test of Wills*, in which Rutledge first hears MacLeod's voice while trying to solve the murder of a village squire.

KEY AUTHORS: HISTORY WITH A DASH OF HUMOR

History doesn't have to be as dull as dirt, and writing a well-researched and vividly detailed historical mystery series doesn't mean that you can't have a sense of humor, as this trio of historical mystery authors demonstrates.

Elizabeth Peters

Elizabeth Peters might have won the race between Ellis Peters and Anne Perry to be the first to see her historical mystery series in print, with the publication of *The Crocodile on the Sandbank*, which debuted in 1975, but it was six years later before Peters delivered the second installment, *The Curse of the Pharaohs*, in her Amelia Peabody Emerson books. Before turning to historical crime, Peters wrote a number of excellent contemporary and historical romantic suspense novels both as Elizabeth Peters and as Barbara Michaels, but she is best known for her Peabody books. Set in the late Victorian era, the books have the same vivid sense of time and place found in Anne Perry's mysteries, but the tone of Peters's books is much lighter and more humorous than Perry's often darker-tinged novels. The series's intrepid heroine first meets archeologist Radcliffe Emerson, who is excavating in Egypt, in *The Crocodile in the Sandbank*, and before long the two are married and starting a family. Not only does Peters perfectly capture the literary flavor of novels written during the late Victorian era in her Amelia Peabody books, but *The Last Camel Died at Noon*, in which Amelia finds herself stuck in the Egyptian desert with her husband and young son while searching for a missing English aristocrat and his wife, is a loving tribute to Victorian adventure novelist Sir Henry Rider Haggard. History, humor, and a dash of romance—what more could a mystery reader ask for?

NOW READ: Suzanne Arruda

Readers who have fallen for Elizabeth Peters's Peabody books will definitely want to give Suzanne Arruda's Jade Del Cameron mysteries a try, as they deliver the same strongly opinionated, no-nonsense female detective, whose personal life abounds with romantic complications, colorful historical setting, and action-rich mystery plots. In the first book of the series, *Mark of the Lion*, Jade, an American who drove an ambulance during World War I, promises her dying fiancé that she will find his brother, but the trail leads Jade to British East Africa, where she runs into murder and the handsome American pilot Sam Featherstone.

Carola Dunn

Carola Dunn is another mystery writer who manages to successfully mix humor with an impeccable sense of history. A former Regency romance novelist, Dunn currently writes a charming series featuring 1920s British flapper turned journalist Daisy Dalrymple, who sleuths her way through a number of fascinating cases, beginning with *Death at Wentwater Court*, and manages to find herself a husband along the way in the form of Detective Chief Inspector Alan Fletcher of Scotland Yard. In many ways the light tone of Dunn's series perfectly complements the cheerier aspects of the 1920s era in which they are set.

NOW READ: Rhys Bowen

Bowen, one of the pseudonyms for author Janet Lee, has written several different exceptionally entertaining series, including the Constable Evan Evans books and the Molly Murphy mysteries, but we think her Royal books featuring Lady Victoria Georgiana Charlotte Eugenie are the perfect read-alike for Carola Dunn's Daisy Dalrymple books. When her family allowance is cut off, Georgie, who is thirty-fourth in line for the British throne, is forced to find a way to earn a living. Written in the same bright and breezy tone as Dunn's mysteries, much of the humor in the Georgie series comes from the protagonist's efforts to find a suitable job that will keep her bank account in the black. Much as Dunn has done, Bowen adds romance to the mix in the person of a sexy Irishman who keeps crossing paths with Georgie. *Her Royal Spyness*, the first in the series, is an excellent place to start, as it introduces readers to Georgie, who after starting her own maid service, stumbles across the body of a drowned man in her bathtub.

Lindsey Davis

Although she never originally intended on writing about ancient Rome, many mystery readers are delighted that Lindsey Davis ultimately decided to set her historical series in the Eternal City circa A.D. 70 because she brings a much-needed sense of humor to the often bloody and brutal era of the Roman Empire. Featuring informer and imperial agent Marcus Didius Falco, the series begins with *The Silver Pigs*, in which Falco is hired to investigate the disappearance of a senator's niece. Throughout the books readers are treated to a number of cleverly constructed mysteries set around the Roman Empire and to the story of Falco's romance with (and eventual marriage to) upper-class Roman citizen Helena Justina. In addition to deftly giving readers a vivid idea of life in imperial Rome, Davis's writing manages to effectively blend the snappy tone of the classic 1930s private investigator (think Sam Spade in sandals) with a colorful, classic setting, which gives the series its uniquely entertaining literary flavor.

NOW READ: Ruth Downie

After your readers have finished everything by Davis, steer them toward Ruth Downie's series featuring military doctor Gaius Petreius Ruso for the same irresistible combination of entertaining characters and a colorfully detailed ancient Roman setting. Like Davis, Downie has a gift for effectively translating the customs and culture of the Roman Empire for modern-day readers without sacrificing historical accuracy, and her writing has the same spike of wry wit found in Davis's Falco mysteries. Give readers *Medicus*, the first in the series, in which Ruso, who is stuck serving in a military hospital in the British port of Deva, finds himself investigating the mysterious deaths of several local working girls, and you can be certain they will be back for more.

8

GENRE-BLENDED MYSTERIES
Torn between Two Genres

One of the hottest trends affecting readers' advisory work today is the blurring between fiction genres. Because mystery fiction is no exception to this literary force, knowing something about how this development affects mystery readers is important even if these mixed-up mysteries don't actually qualify as a separate subgenre of their own.

Although the concept of a detective story that blends genres might seem to be a recent one, in reality these types of mysteries have been around for decades. Beginning with his 1954 book *Caves of Steel*, science fiction writer Isaac Asimov introduced readers to the idea of a robot detective. Fantasy and mystery readers both know author Randall Garrett for his acclaimed Lord Darcy series, which deftly distills elements of magic and murder into inventive tales of mystery. John Dickson Carr wrote dozens of traditional, classic mysteries, but he also authored several genre-blurring detective stories, including one often called his masterpiece, *The Burning Court*. In this brilliantly subtle story, first published in 1937, a man discovers that his wife has the same name as and looks exactly like a notorious poisoner who was executed for her crimes nearly a century earlier. When several people suddenly begin dying from poison—the same type that nineteenth-century murderess used—what is the man to think?

Western fiction and mysteries have cross-pollinated one another with interesting results for decades. This really is not as surprising as it might first seem, as both fiction genres focus on the triumph of justice and the restoration of law and order to society. Western writer James Warner Bellah's 1960 book *Sergeant Rutledge* features a buffalo soldier who is charged with double assault and homicide and must find the real killer to clear his name. Award-winning mystery writer Bill Pronzini achieved an almost-perfect combination of the western and mystery genres with his book *Quincannon*, and Bill Crider, another mystery writer who also authors westerns, has several genre-blurred books, including *Ryan Rides Back*. Best-selling writer Tony Hillerman's *Skinwalkers* not only won the Anthony Award for Best Mystery but also garnered the Golden Spur Award from the Western Writers of America for Best Western Novel, thus proving that critics of both genres know a good book when they read it.

Even literary fiction is not immune to the appeal of the mystery genre. Margaret Atwood's *Alias Grace*, David Guterson's *Snow Falling on Cedars*, Jodi Picoult's *Plain Truth*, and Kate Morton's *The House at Riverton* are just a few examples of literary fiction writers who have added everything from a pinch to a generous measure of mystery to their stories. Interestingly enough, some literary fiction readers are discovering that many mystery writers, such as Sharyn McCrumb, P. D. James, and James Lee Burke, have distinctive literary voices and that their books can be enjoyed for both the prose and the puzzle.

For those who believe in keeping books in neat and tidy categories, genre-blurred mysteries can be a real trial. But they do have some advantages, one being that they give readers' advisory staff an easy way to introduce the mystery genre to readers who might not pick up a detective story on their own. Conversely, when you give a genre-blended mystery to mystery readers, you might also give them a gentle push into trying another type of book, such as a fantasy novel. Think of genre-blended mysteries as not only offering the opportunity to cross-market your mystery collection to new readers but also as a way to steer your mystery readers into another section of your library's stacks that they might enjoy.

With the constant evolution of new variations of genre-blurred books, choosing just a few examples isn't easy, but here are some authors and titles to get you started.

ELVES PACKING HEAT: FANTASY DETECTION

Blending two different fiction genres is difficult to do, but with his Dresden Files books the author Jim Butcher successfully merges the hard-boiled private-eye mystery with the fantasy genre. Butcher's books feature Chicago-based wizard and private detective Harry Dresden, who in the series debut, *Storm Front*, takes on a case of a missing husband only to become involved in a series of murders by magic. Throughout the series, Harry not only solves real-world murders and crimes but also must deal with unreal power struggles among the different factions (vampires, "faeries," and wizards) battling for control of the world. Butcher creates exceptionally entertaining characters and excels at capturing the cynical, wise-cracking tone of the classic private-eye novel, which makes his Dresden Files books read something like a cross between Dashiell Hammett's Sam Spade and Continental Op mysteries and Terry Pratchett's wildly imaginative Discworld books.

Glen Cook has written a number of fantasy series, but his eleven books featuring Garrett, a private investigator whose cases involve fantasy creatures, belong in any mystery collection. Imagine Raymond Chandler's Phillip Marlowe transported to a world created by J. R. R. Tolkien, and you have an idea of the flavor of Glenn Cook's Garrett series, which begins with *Sweet Silver Blues*. The Garrett books work well for both mystery and fantasy readers because Cook not only knows how to write the traditional hard-boiled private detective novel but also brings the world-building skills of an expert fantasy writer to the series.

Few writers are as deft when it comes to blending genres as Jasper Fforde. With his Thursday Next books, Fforde has a created an alternate universe—Great Britain circa 1985—in which the Crimean War is still being fought, and animals such as the dodo never died out. The series protagonist is Thursday Next, a special operative in literary detection, who tracks criminals in and out of books. In *The Eyre Affair*, the first book in the series, Thursday must find out who is murdering characters in the great works of British literature (once a character is killed, his or her book also ceases to exist) before he can do away with Jane Eyre. In addition to his Thursday Next novels, Fforde has also written two books in his Nursery Crime series, set in a wildly inventive world where nursery-rhyme characters such as Detective Inspector Jack Spratt really exist. The books cleverly spoof the hard-boiled style of detective fiction while delivering all the wickedly sharp humor to which Fforde's readers have become addicted.

ROMANCE MEETS MURDER: DEADLY DAMES AND KILLER KISSES

It shouldn't be surprising that there is a strong thread of romance woven into the In Death series written by J. D. Robb, as Robb is the pseudonym for best-selling romance writer Nora Roberts. Set in twenty-first-century New York, the series stars NYPD lieutenant Eve Dallas and her husband, mysterious Irish billionaire Roarke. Eve first meets Roarke in *Naked in Death*, when Roarke is a suspect in the murder of high-priced, high-class prostitute. As the series progress, Eve and Roarke fall in love and eventually marry, and their strongly romantic (and passionately sexy) relationship provides the glue that holds this long-running series together. Although there is a potent measure of romance to the In Death books, Robb's novels are also solidly constructed, realistically gritty procedural mysteries, with Eve and her team of officers using traditional police methods of detection—with the occasional futuristic twist—to solve crimes. In short, J. D. Robb's books are the perfect mix of romance and mystery.

With its charming blend of sweet romance and genial mystery, author C. A. Belmond's Rather series can be thought of as a modern update on Hammett's classic *The Thin Man*. *A Rather Lovely Inheritance* introduces readers to Penny Nichols, an American freelance historical researcher, who has just learned that her incredibly wealthy great-aunt Penelope has died and named Penny in her will. When Penny arrives in England, she discovers that her great-aunt's estate is to be split between her cousin Rollo and another "cousin," Jeremy Laidley. When Penny and Jeremy team up together against Rollo (who is contesting the will), they find themselves falling in love. As the series continues with *A Rather Charming Invitation* and *A Rather Curious Engagement*, both a personal relationship and a professional relationship are forged between Penny and Jeremy, who work together to solve cases involving missing yachts and valuable tapestries. It all sounds a bit like *Lifestyles of the Rich and Famous* meets *Globe Trekker*, but Belmond manages to maintain the delicate balance between romance and mystery (and high-class travelogue), which makes the Rather books a wonderful introduction to the mystery genre for old-fashioned romance readers.

SHERLOCK HOLMES VERSUS DR. FRANKENSTEIN: HORROR TAKES ON MYSTERY

Long before the vampire phenomena hit the publishing world, Tanya Huff wrote a quartet of wonderfully clever books about Henry Fitzroy, the bastard son of Henry VIII and a romance-writing, four-hundred-year-old vampire, Victoria Nelson, a retired city cop turned private eye, and Michael Celluci, a Toronto police sergeant, who team up to solve murders involving werewolves, mummies, and zombies. The quartet of books begins with *Blood Price*, in which a demon called up by a college student goes on a killing spree, and the three must work together to stop it. Throughout the series Huff demonstrates a real gift for mixing horror, mystery, and even romance.

Although Laurell K. Hamilton's series featuring Anita Blake, Vampire Hunter, is all about vampires, werewolves, and shapeshifters (oh my!), there is also a strong thread of detection—and plenty of steamy romance—in the books, enough so that the Anita Blake books are a good suggestion for mystery readers who want to give the horror genre a try. In the first book in the series, *Guilty Pleasures*, Anita, a licensed vampire executioner, finds herself not only investigating a string of vampire murders but also dealing with two equally sexy (and equally dangerous) men. As the series progresses, Hamilton turns up the sensual heat to full boil as Anita becomes involved with master vampire Jean-Claude while still sorting out her relationship with her ex-fiancé (and werewolf) Richard. In addition, Anita goes from just moonlighting as a vampire killer to actively teaming up with city and federal agents investigating supernatural crimes. If your readers become hooked with the series (and it can be addictive), Hamilton also writes another hot and steamy series featuring Merry Gentry, a half-mortal and half-fairy princess who works as a magic consultant for an LA detective agency.

Kim Harrison's Rachel Morgan books are an engaging mix of horror, mystery, and fantasy. The series is set in a world in which a virus carried in a genetically altered tomato has killed all humans, and the only survivors are those who are supernatural in some way: vampires, witches, elves, demons. In *Dead Witch Walking*, the first in the series, Morgan, a supernatural bounty hunter and witch, decides to quit working for the Inderland Security organization and open her own private detective agency. The books' fast-paced, danger-infused plots and sharp, snappy writing style work as great readers' advisory hooks, but start readers off with *Dead Witch Walking* so they can get the full effect of this bewitching and utterly addictive series.

THE PAST IS ANOTHER MYSTERY: HISTORICAL FICTION AND THE CRIME NOVEL

Iain Pears began his writing career with a series of contemporary art and antiquities mysteries featuring British art dealer Jonathan Argyll and his paramour and partner in detection, Flavia de Stefano, of the Italian National Art Theft Squad. It is two of Pears recent novels, *An Instance of the Fingerpost* and *Stone's Fall*, however, which serve as an excellent introduction to the mystery genre for historical fiction fans. Set in 1660s England, *An Instance of the Fingerpost* is the story of the murder of Oxford scholar

Robert Grove, told from the viewpoints of five different main characters. Each one gives his or her account of the event, leaving the reader to guess as to which parts of their story are true and which are red herrings. *An Instance of a Fingerpost* transports readers to the world of Restoration England, providing the luxuriously detailed settings and large cast of characters that historical fiction fans crave while also offering a cleverly constructed tale of murder. *Stone's Fall* opens in 1909 with the death of British financier John Stone, a death some think might not have been the accident it seems to be. After Stone's widow, Elizabeth, discovers that her late husband left a portion of the estate to an heir she never knew existed, she hires journalist Matthew Braddock to find the heir. Leisurely working its way backward in time from Edwardian England to 1890s Paris and finally to Venice in 1867, *Stone's Fall* transports mystery readers to another time and place while giving historical fiction readers a richly rewarding tale of subtle suspense and deadly intrigue.

Ariana Franklin was the pseudonym for journalist turned author Diana Norman. After writing several nonfiction works and a half dozen historical novels, *City of Shadows*, Norman's first book as Franklin, was published in 2005. Set in 1920s and 1930s Berlin, the book centers on Anna Anderson, who becomes caught up in a scheme to establish her credentials as the last surviving member of the Romanov family. Franklin's novel *Mistress of the Art of Death* quickly followed and became the first book in a series featuring twelfth-century doctor Adelia Aguilar, who travels from Italy to England, where Henry II hires her to find out who is behind a series of gruesome murders being blamed on the Jews in London. More titles in the series followed, with Adelia investigating murders in both castles and convents and dealing with the fallout from her romantic liaison with a nobleman, who is now the bishop of Saint Albans. With each book in the Adelia Aguilar series, Franklin not only flawlessly re-creates the both civilized and brutal world of medieval England but also delivers a cleverly constructed murder, which makes the books the perfect synthesis of mystery and history.

ROUNDING UP SUSPECTS THE WESTERN WAY

If Sir Arthur Conan Doyle and Louis L'Amour teamed up to write a series, the result might be something close to the novels of Steven Hockensmith. First introduced to readers in a short story Hockensmith wrote for *Ellery Queen's Mystery Magazine* in 2003, Otto "Big Red" and Gustave "Old Red"

Amlingmeyer reappeared in their first novel, *Holmes on the Range*, in 2005. After hearing his brother read a Sherlock Holmes story around the campfire, Old Red vows to follow in Holmes's footsteps, getting his first chance when the ranch's general manager is killed in a stampede. With cattle drives and cowboys, puzzling murders, and red herrings, in each new addition to his Amlingmeyer series, Hockensmith mixes elements from both western and mystery genres with colorful flair and a uniquely outrageous sense of humor.

Loren Estleman is known for his award-winning mystery series featuring Detroit-based private investigator Amos Walker, but he has also written a number of classic westerns, of which his Page Murdock series effectively and entertainingly blurs the lines between the two genres. The series begins with *The High Rocks*, in which Montana lawman Murdock tracks down the Indians who killed his parents. As the series progresses, Murdock moves around his Montana base, traveling north to Canada to capture outlaws who killed a settlement of gold prospectors and south to Texas, where he meets up with an old flame. All the elements western readers demand from their genre—a vivid sense of place and time, a strong hero with a iron code of honor, and an action-packed plot—are present in the Page Murdock series, which makes the series an easy sell to both diehard western fans and hard-boiled private-eye readers.

THE FUTURE OF CRIME: SCIENCE FICTION AND MYSTERIES

Best-selling, award-winning author Isaac Asimov is best known for his popular nonfiction books that translate science into everyday English for laypeople and for his numerous groundbreaking science-fiction novels. But Asimov was equally intrigued by puzzles and mysteries, and he authored several Black Widow mysteries in which the members of the Widowers Club meet over dinner to match wits and solve puzzles. With the publication in 1954 of his book *The Caves of Steel*, Asimov fused what he believed to be the best elements of the science fiction and mystery genres. Asimov's popular robot short stories inspired the book, which is set in a future world where humans are divided into two groups. Those who now live on Earth congregate in covered cities—the caves of steel of the title. Spacers are descendants of humans who colonized the Outer Worlds. In *The Caves of Steel*, human police detective Elijah "Lije" Bailey must investigate the murder of a Spacer robot scientist with the help of a robot named R. Daneel Olivaw. The two partners team up again in *The Naked Sun*, in which they travel to the planet Solaria, where they must solve another puzzling murder, and then return once more in *The Robots of the Dawn*. Science, space exploration, and robotics mix with murder, method, and motive in Asimov's three books, which makes this trio of titles a good bet for fans of either fiction genre.

With her brilliantly inventive series featuring District Marshal Ty Merrick and her partner Andy LaRue, Denise Vitola introduces readers to a bleak, *Blade Runner*–like version of the planet Earth struggling with a severe lack of basic resources and social justice and dealing with an abundance of government corruption and corporate greed. *Quantum Moon*, the first in the series, has Ty and Andy investigating the murder of a powerful district councilman's wife. Future cases take the two into the world of secret societies, government espionage and assassins, and a planetary heath spa and rejuvenation facility. Vitola throws in another twist—and a paranormal one at that—by making Ty a lycanthrope, who must deal with the ongoing problems of her condition while struggling to keep her government employers from finding out. In classic noir style, Ty provides the viewpoint for each case, and her world-weary, cynical voice neatly evokes the spirit of the traditional hard-boiled police detective trying to deliver justice in a bleak, futuristic world.

THE SOFTER SIDE OF MURDER: GENTLE READS

Ever since the publication of *The No. 1 Ladies' Detective Agency* in 1998, Alexander McCall Smith's books featuring Mma Precious Ramotswe have been a hit with mystery fans. McCall Smith's Sunday Philosophy Club series, which begins with *The Sunday Philosophy Club* and centers on amateur sleuth and university-trained philosopher Isabel Dalhousie, has gained him even more readers in the mystery genre. Although suggesting these books to cozy mystery readers requires very little thought, as readers' advisors, we sometimes forget that the two series by McCall Smith can work equally well for gentle-reads patrons. Whether in colorful Gaborone (where Precious owns and operates Botswana's best-known and only female-run detective agency) or the more familiar Edinburgh (where Isabel debates life's philosophical questions with her circle of friends), the universal appeal of the books comes from the author's ability to blend the best elements of both fiction genres into one. Both series deliver the charmingly crafted mysteries sans gory violence and graphic language that cozy mystery readers expect, and they offer the endearing characters and quietly compelling storylines that gentle-read fans require. The very best gentle-read books provide a comforting literary antidote to the sometimes-overwhelming stresses and strains of the modern world, and McCall Smith's are very good at leaving readers with a wonderful feeling of literary satisfaction and domestic well-being.

Well, there you have it: our choices for some popular genre-blurring authors and titles. We are certain even as this book is being read (or not), new strains of genre-blended novels are being written and published, providing readers' advisory staff with even more cross-marketing possibilities, and adventurous readers with even more great books from which to choose.

9

THE MYSTERY READERS' ADVISORY INTERVIEW

The key ingredient in most successful readers' advisory transactions is the readers' advisory interview. All library staff who provide readers' advisory service should be familiar with the standard text on the subject: Joyce G. Saricks's *Readers' Advisory Service in the Public Library.* Saricks's book brilliantly covers all the basic elements required in any readers' advisory interview, but in this chapter we focus on readers' advisory interview factors unique to the mystery genre.

The minute they begin talking with us, mystery readers give us many valuable clues about what kind of book they enjoy. For example, the reader who says they devour fast-paced procedural stories will probably not appreciate a leisurely paced amateur sleuth book. The lady who says she loves Sue Grafton's Kinsey Millhone books because she enjoys following Kinsey's adventures is also probably telling you that she would rather have a mystery that is part of a series rather than a stand-alone title. Encouraging readers to talk about what they enjoy and dislike about the mysteries they are currently reading is the first step in getting a better idea of what book might next work for them.

There are a number of factors to consider when working with mystery readers, from the amount of violence in the story to the focus—character or plot—of the mystery itself. For every reader, some elements will be more important than others. Discovering which of these factors is of key importance to the individual mystery reader is crucial when it comes to creating a rewarding readers' advisory interaction.

The most important factor in working with mystery readers is to be sure you are both talking about the same kind of books. As discussed earlier in our book, we define mystery fiction separately from suspense novels and thrillers. But not every reader may use this decisive dividing line.

For some readers, mysteries mean books by Mary Higgins Clark or Mary Stewart. As library staff, we might catalog these authors as suspense writers, which means switching readers' advisory gears a bit when working with these readers.

Every fiction genre seems to have its own particular issue that must be taken into account when it comes to working with readers. In the romance genre, it is the amount of sensuality in the story with which the reader feels comfortable. In the mystery genre, the question is how much violence—and to a lesser degree, graphic language and sex—is acceptable to the reader. As you begin working with mystery readers, you will quickly find that their comfort levels for graphic violence, language, and sex vary greatly. Finding a way to introduce this into the readers' advisory interview gracefully is not always easy.

Fortunately for us, readers often give us this information without us even having to ask. When readers use terms such as *cozy*, *traditional*, *hard boiled*, and even *noir* in describing the types of mysteries they enjoy reading, they are giving you a clear hint as to the levels of graphic violence and language that they find acceptable. To understand how these qualifiers play into the mystery readers' advisory interview, let's take a moment and discuss these terms.

COZY IS NOT A FOUR-LETTER WORD

The term *cozy* was first traced to a mystery review published in 1958, and over the following decades, it has come to define a certain type of mystery for many readers.[1] Used on its own, cozy does not really represent a unique mystery subgenre. After all, cozy mysteries can be found in all of the mystery subgenres, but the word has come to mean several things for mystery readers. Most important, in a cozy mystery, the murder either takes place offstage or is described in such a way in the book that the reader does not receive graphic details about the crime. Violence is kept to a minimum in a cozy mystery, and these books have a gentle literary flavor and a sense of civilized refinement. In almost all cozy mysteries, the murder takes place in a closed environment, such as a country house, a small village, or an office. Most of the characters in a cozy know one another and have some connection to the crime. In a cozy, murder disrupts the sense of order that prevails in these characters' world, and it is only when the crime is solved that order is restored. Psychopathic serial killers do not stalk victims in a cozy mystery, and Patricia Cornwell has yet to write a cozy crime novel.

However, simply using the word *cozy* to describe a mystery can be confusing, because the word can mean different things to different readers. For some, the term *cozy* conjures up images of a small English village in which a spinster sleuths her way through a variety of civilized murders. These readers might be a bit surprised when offered a series such as Chris Cavender's Pizza Lovers books. Featuring amateur sleuth and recent widower Eleanor Swift, owner of A Slice of Delight, and her sister Maddy, the books are set in the small town of Timber Ridge, North Carolina, and seem worlds away from Miss Marple and St. Mary's Mead. Yet Cavender's books have many of the same cozy components—including an enclosed circle of suspects, a minimum of graphic violence and language, and a cleverly constructed, puzzle-based plot—found in their British counterparts.

It should be no surprise that most cozies do come from the amateur sleuth subgenre, but there are plenty of cozies in other mystery subgenres, too. M. C. Beaton's Hamish Macbeth books and Rhys Bowen's Evans series are terrific examples of wonderfully cozy police procedural series. Newcomer Tarquin Hall has two private-eye books (with the promise of more) in his new cozy series featuring Vish Puri, the Indian owner and founder of Most Private Investigations. Carola Dunn and K. K. Beck have written charmingly cozy historical mysteries. There are even cozies without human detectives, such as Leonie Swann's wonderfully clever *Three Bags Full: A Sheep Detective Agency*, in which a flock of sheep led by a wooly Miss Maple solve the mystery of who killed their shepherd. When readers say that they enjoy a cozy mystery, they are in effect simply telling you something about the level of graphic violence they will permit in her mystery fiction. What they are not saying is that they read only one subgenre of mysteries.

A CLASSIC NEVER GOES OUT OF STYLE

What can be equally challenging is that some mystery readers use the term *cozy* to mean the classic, traditional type of mystery written by authors such as Dorothy L. Sayers, Ngaio Marsh, and Patricia Wentworth. Many of the classic British and American mystery writers of the 1920s and 1930s wrote books that share characteristics with today's contemporary cozy mysteries, such as the civilized sense of atmosphere and lack of graphic violence, even though their sleuths are often professional police detectives, such as Ngaio Marsh's Inspector Roderick Alleyn, instead of the typical amateur sleuth found in most contemporary cozies. These readers will be delighted when you introduce them to an author such as G. M. Malliet, whose series featuring Detective Chief Inspector St. Just is a wonderful, modern interpretation of Golden Age mystery masterpieces.

It might seem that everyone in the world has already read mystery authors such as Rex Stout and Josephine Tey, but the reality is that many readers new to the mystery genre have yet to discover the classics. Introducing a reader to one of the greats of the mystery world is always a delight, but it is important to remember when suggesting classic mysteries that they were written during a different time and place. Phrases, words, and even views on different cultures and classes that were acceptable then in society might be less politically correct today, and some readers might find this a stumbling block when reading a book written decades ago. Every book is a product of the time in which it was written. Keeping this in mind—and letting readers know this fact—is an additional thing to take into account when conducting a readers' advisory interview.

HARD BOILED, SOFT BOILED: WHAT DO EGGS HAVE TO DO WITH MYSTERIES?

Although some mystery readers relish a good cozy, others want us to recommend a terrific hard-boiled detective novel. Once again, readers, in using a term such as this, are giving you a clue as to how much violence they tolerate in their choice of mystery.

Just as *cozy* has often come to signify the amateur sleuth subgenre for some readers, *hard boiled* is most often used in reference to the private-investigator subgenre of mysteries. The protagonist in a hard-boiled detective novel is usually a tough loner, someone who is at odds with the world. This is an immediate contrast to the cozy sleuth, who is tied into a community and who is part of a close-knit circle of family, friends, and acquaintances. Most hard-boiled mysteries take place in an urban setting, and there is an attempt on the part of the author to give readers a realistically gritty look at murder. Corruption and violence are often a part of the hard-boiled sleuth's world. In a hard-boiled mystery, action and violence are an integral part of the story, but they are never used as a shortcut for character development. Just as some readers love the quaint tone and atmosphere of a good cozy, others delight in the unique literary flavor of the hard-boiled world.

In the 1930s and 1940s, private-eye novelists such as Dashiell Hammett, Raymond Chandler, and Mickey Spillane in many ways shaped and defined the hard-boiled detective story. However, with the arrival of female mystery writers such as Marcia Muller and Sue Grafton on the private-eye scene, a new term for the level of violence was needed. Thus, *soft boiled* came into literary use to define these (almost-always) private detective novels, which shared many characteristics with their classic male counterparts but in which the level of graphic violence and language was softened.

A reader who loves Grafton's Kinsey Millhone books may also enjoy other soft-boiled series by authors such as Linda Barnes, Marcia Muller, and Sandi Ault, but the same reader might reject grittier, more hard-boiled mysteries by an author such as Dennis Lehane or the modern noir novels of Megan Abbott. Just as there are those people who want their eggs fixed in different ways, there are readers who choose the level of and graphic language in their mystery books, from hard boiled to soft boiled.

NOIR: BLACK IS ALWAYS IN FASHION

In addition to the use of *hard boiled* and *soft boiled* to describe mysteries, you may also hear readers use the term *noir*. Some critics consider noir mysteries to be just another type of hard-boiled private detective story. Both hard-boiled and noir mysteries can have high levels of graphic violence and language, but there are some differences in the two terms. Noir mysteries, including those written by James M. Cain and Cornell Woolrich, often do not feature a private eye as the story's protagonist. In a noir mystery, there is a general overall feeling of despair and bleakness. Even if a hard-boiled detective lives in a corrupt world, there is at least the expectation that some form of justice will prevail in the end, but that is not always the case with noir fiction. Noir is all about mood and atmosphere.

MORE OF WHAT MYSTERY READERS WANT: CHARACTER, PLOT, OR A LITTLE OF BOTH

Another important topic that should be discussed during the readers' advisory interview is whether the reader enjoys a character-driven or a plot-driven mystery. In a character-driven mystery, the focus is on the story's protagonist; plot-driven mysteries center more on solving the crime in the book. An easy way to think of this distinction is whether the reader cares more about the detective in the story or whether following the clues to the identity of the villain is more important.

Perhaps the most extreme examples of plot-driven mysteries can be found among books published during the Golden Age of mystery fiction, from the 1920s to the 1940s. In some of these books, readers were given a puzzle to solve, and they had to scrutinize everything from train schedules to floor plans if they were to have any hope of beating the detective to the solution of the mystery. One of the best examples of a puzzle-centered author is Freeman Wills Crofts, whose series featuring Inspector Joseph French almost always has the British police officer scouring train timetables in an effort to figure out how to break a suspect's unbreakable alibi. Conversely, extreme examples of character-driven mysteries are sometimes found among the crop of detective novels published in the past decade. Some contemporary mystery writers dedicate so much space in their books to cataloging their protagonist's career, relationships, hobbies, and so on, that the mystery itself gets lost in all these personal details. For some readers an example of this might be a certain best-selling series featuring a New Jersey bounty hunter in which the mystery becomes only a frame for the ongoing adventures of the protagonist and her colorful friends and family.

Most mysteries fall somewhere in between these two ends of the literary spectrum. The very best mysteries balance the twin demands of creating a compelling cast of characters with the challenge of working out an intriguing puzzle.

One danger we readers' advisors must be on alert for is stereotyping readers. A sweet, grandmotherly lady comes to the desk and asks for a "good" mystery. Immediately, we think of authors such as Charlotte MacLeod or Virginia Rich; in reality, however, she wants the latest John Sanford or Stieg Larsson. "Certainly that man looking through a copy of the best-seller list wants to reserve the latest Michael Connelly," we think to ourselves when, much to our surprise, he wants to the latest Diane Mott Davidson. It can take awhile to dismantle our preconceived notions about readers, but the first step is to listen to readers first before guessing what we think they want.

Occasionally, you will find a mystery fan who reads for a certain theme, such as art mysteries, culinary mysteries, or mysteries set in Italy. Nothing else matters as much to this reader as the fact that the book be structured around certain plot elements. Other elements that might be important, including subgenre, matter less than having key elements present in the story. Fortunately, there are several mystery reference works and at least one mystery magazine, *Mystery Readers Journal*, that can help you locate mysteries centered on a certain theme.

I WANT ANOTHER ONE . . . : THE APPEAL OF A SERIES

The whole question of a series is yet another thing you must keep in mind when chatting with readers about the type of mystery they enjoy. Series are an important part of the mystery genre, and they have certain characteristics that appeal to many readers (as well as authors and publishers). Some readers delight in discovering a new mystery series. After all, it means that if they enjoy the first book they read, they have many more in the series.

Mystery series do introduce some new challenges into the readers' advisory interview. Some readers insist on starting a series at the beginning, believing that picking up a book in the middle of a series is like entering a conversation that began before they arrived. This is one point you will need to clarify when talking with a mystery reader. In some cases, even if it doesn't matter to the reader, a series is best read in order. For example, someone who starts Dana Stabenow's Kate Shugak series with *Hunter's Moon*, the ninth title in the series, will find that the book contains a dramatic plot twist that changes everything that came before it in the series. Reading the earlier books in the series might be less satisfying for some readers if they know what happens in *Hunter's Moon*. Another example is Elizabeth George's British procedural series featuring Inspector Thomas Lynley and Sergeant Barbara Havers. Over the course of the series, George has changed the personal dynamics between many of the characters so much that readers who pick up the latest book without knowing anything of her main detective's pasts will not have as richly rewarding a reading experience as those who start the series at the beginning.

In other series, such as the John Putnam Thatcher mysteries written by Emma Lathen, readers can read and enjoy books in any order because the series sleuth does not change significantly from book to book; the focus in this series is on the individual business settings and the classically constructed plots rather than the life of the detective. Another example of this are the Hercule Poirot mysteries by Agatha Christie. With the exception of the final Poirot book, *Curtain*, in which Christie plays a cunning final trick on the reader, the Poirot mysteries can be read and enjoyed in any order.

Not only is dealing with a mystery series a challenge to library staff; it can also present some unique hurdles for authors themselves. After all, how do you introduce a regular series character in your latest title to a reader who is just beginning your books without at the same time boring readers who have been with you from the start? How do you keep a series fresh and original after the fifth book, the tenth book, and even the twentieth book? Despite these challenges, writing a series does provide an author with the opportunity to develop a character over time and to really explore his or her life without impacting the mystery du jour. Of course, it goes without saying that publishers love a mystery series: they are easy to package and market, and there is the implicit guarantee that the latest title is already "presold" to a certain number of readers.

Series are such an important part of the mystery genre that some series keep going long after the original author has left the earthly plane. This was the case with the English village mysteries featuring Miss Seeton, which were originally written by Heron Carvic. After his death, James Melville took over writing the books as Hampton Charles, and later Sarah J. Mason picked up the series as Hamilton Crane. Robert Goldsborough wrote several Nero Wolfe mysteries much to the readers' delight (or annoyance, depending on the reader) long after Rex Stout was gone. Jill Paton Walsh not only finished one uncompleted Lord Peter Wimsey book started by Dorothy L. Sayers but also went on to write two more new and completely original Wimsey mysteries "based on the characters of Dorothy L. Sayers." These are just a few examples of the enduring appeal of a series. When it comes to a series, the best advice we can offer is, when in doubt, start the reader with the first book your library might have in that series.

WHOLE-COLLECTION MYSTERY READERS' ADVISORY WORK

It is easy when working with readers to think of readers' advisory only in terms of the "book" but the reality is that readers' advisory service is not just a "print" thing. In this section, we will talk about expanding your mystery readers' advisory work into your audio/visual collection.

Some of the basic mystery readers' advisory considerations, such as the amount of graphic language or violence readers want in their story, apply no matter the format. But formats other than the printed book do have a few unique readers' advisory elements that need to be considered. When it comes to working with your spoken-word or audio mystery fans, one of the most important questions to ask is, Abridged or unabridged? Some listeners will take an audiobook only if it is the word-for-word equivalent of the book (i.e., unabridged), whereas others will listen to anything as long as the adaptation is good.

Another factor to take into account is the narrator of the individual audiobook. Some readers are fanatically devoted to certain narrators, and this becomes a factor in helping them find their next title. This dedication to a specific narrator does have one advantage for you as the readers' advisor, as you can often introduce readers to a mystery subgenre they might not ordinarily listen to if the narrator is one of their favorites. One difficulty in audio readers' advisory (no matter the genre) is that not every book is also available in audio format.

When it comes to mysteries on film, there are some other readers' advisory twists to factor in. Many classic and contemporary mysteries have been successfully translated into movies, but one of the first things to discuss with your patron is how true to the original story the movie must be for him or her. In cases where one book has inspired a number of film versions, you can ask whether there is one in particular that the reader is looking for. And how true to the book does the movie have to be for it to succeed with this viewer? For example, *The Maltese Falcon* has been filmed several times (including a version with Bette Davis), but most people want the classic Humphrey Bogart version to watch.

Agatha Christie's Miss Marple books have seen several screen adaptations, including four 1960s movies featuring Margaret Rutherford, several made-for-television movies starring legendary Broadway star Helen Hays and Angela Lansbury (whose performance is said to have inspired the creation of the television series *Murder She Wrote*), a PBS series featuring Joan Hickson, and more recent PBS versions starring both Geraldine McEwan and Julia McKenzie. Some mystery readers will enjoy any and all of these versions, but for others, Joan Hickson's version of Miss Marple is the only acceptable one, especially because several of the other Marple adaptations, most notably the Margaret Rutherford and the Julia McKenzie ones, took some great liberties with the books (in some cases even borrowing plots from other Christie novels).

Another thing to keep in mind when working with mystery film fans is that not all movies have a literary equivalent. For example, the Midsomer Murders series is based on characters created by author Caroline Graham for her traditional British police procedural mysteries. But the majority of television movies are original screenplays, so the viewer who devoured the film version and now wants its book equivalent will not find it. The same is true with the PBS adaptations of Elizabeth George's books. The first episodes in the series were based on George's books featuring Chief Inspector Thomas Lynley and Detective Barbara Havers, but PBS has since gone on to produce a number of equally entertaining episodes based on original screenplays. The new Inspector Lewis series is another example. The title character is based on a secondary character from Colin Dexter's Inspector Morse books (which themselves were later turned into a PBS series), and this series has no print equivalent.

Sometimes the book and the film versions of a mystery series are quite different. Those who loved the witty and romantic *Lovejoy* series that once played on A&E and are now available on DVD will find Jonathan Gash's books featuring the antiques dealer to be quite different in tone. And sometimes there is simply no book equivalent for a terrific mystery series. For example, the British mystery series *Rosemary and Thyme* ran for several years on BBC, then made its way to the United States, and now is available on DVD. The show features two middle-age female sleuths whose knowledge of gardening and botany helps them solve a number of puzzling murders. A couple of novels based on the characters eventually were published, but the cozy and charming series works best as a dramatic production.

CROSSING OVER TO NONFICTION

Although readers' advisory staff might think the idea of steering readers from fiction to nonfiction is a new development, it has actually been part of the mystery readers' advisors' toolkit for decades in the form of true crime. It is true that most mystery readers' advisory work is dedicated to fiction, but true-crime books are an important part of the spectrum of choices open to the mystery reader. But true-crime books can provoke strong reactions: some readers cannot get enough of them, and other readers won't touch them with a ten-foot pole.

Books about true crimes have been popular with readers ever since Truman Capote's *In Cold Blood* became a bestseller in 1966. *In Cold Blood* was followed by subsequent best sellers by other authors, such as *Helter Skelter*, *The Boston Strangler*, *Nutcracker: Money, Madness, and Murder*, and *Fatal Vision*, to name just a few. As these titles demonstrate, there is a distinct range of books in the true-crime category, including the more literary approaches such as Capote's book and Ann Rule's thoughtful, in-depth analyses and the more sensationalistic, *National Enquirer* kind of book that appears almost immediately after a celebrity crime hits the front page.

What draws some readers to true-crime books? The strongest appeal element may be the need to understand why some people turn into cold-blooded killers and others do not. What is it that can make a seemingly normal person become a deranged murderer? Another reason true-crime books are a hit with readers is that some very popular authors, including Edna Buchanan, Patricia Cornwell, Joseph Wambaugh, and James Ellroy, have written both mystery fiction and true-crime nonfiction, and their readers follow them back and forth across the genres.

Although true-crime books are nonfiction, for many of their fans, the best examples of the subgenre read like fiction. This presents the opportunity for readers' advisory staff to cross-sell the books to many mystery fiction readers. For example, fans of police procedurals will find that many true-crime writers devote a considerable portion of their books to following the official investigation of the crime and narrating how the police or other government agencies nab their killer. These kinds of technical insider details are exactly what many procedural fans want in their fictional mysteries. Historical mystery readers will find any number of true-crime books that focus on a crime from the past, such as the perennially popular Jack the Ripper or Erik Larson's stunning historical nonfiction crime books *Devil in the White City* and *Thunderstruck*, and these books deliver the same fascinating details about another time and place found in a historical mystery.

True crime isn't the only kind of nonfiction mystery readers might enjoy, though. Biographies and autobiographies of authors are one easy way to introduction your mystery readers to the world of nonfiction. Biographies of authors, such as Janet Morgan's excellent *Agatha Christie* or Diane Johnson's *Dashiell Hammett*, can be terrific entertainment and give readers new insights to their favorite authors. Several mystery authors, including Ngaio Marsh and Tony Hillerman, have written their own autobiographies, which offer readers an unequaled opportunity to learn more about their lives and books.

Literary criticism is another section to which you can steer some mystery readers. Reading about the mystery genre in a book such as Julian Symon's classic *Bloody Words* can be very rewarding (in addition to giving the reader examples of new authors to try). Readers of P. D. James will be thrilled that their favorite author has also written her own survey of the mystery genre: *Talking about Detective Fiction.* Although the title itself could use some work, the book gives detective fans a good idea of why James writes detective fiction and what she considers the most important contributions in the genre. Fans of Agatha Christie will definitely want to give Robert Barnard's book *A Talent to Deceive* a try. Barnard, an award-winning mystery novelist himself, writes with wit and enthusiasm about Christie's books, clearly giving readers an idea of her legendary place in the genre. Anne Hart wrote two wonderful "biographies" of Christie's most popular sleuths: *The Life and Times of Hercule Poirot* and *The Life and Times of Miss Jane Marple*, both of which provide a great deal of insight into the two characters.

One important thing to remember as you direct readers to nonfiction works such as literary criticism and author biographies is that some of these books go into considerable detail about the author's novels, including providing the solution to the crime, so many readers will want to wait until they have finished an author's literary oeuvre before venturing over into nonfiction.

When it comes to working with mystery readers, we have discovered two useful tips to add to your readers' advisory tool kit. First, give the reader a couple of choices when it comes to suggested titles. Remember, if they don't enjoy one mystery, then they will have another title that might be a better literary fit. Second, don't forget that some authors write under several pseudonyms, and many readers will want to try all of an author's works no matter which name is actually on the cover.

When providing readers' advisory services, remember that doing so is still more of an art than a science. The mystery readers' advisory interview can be both challenging and rewarding, but as long as you follow the clues we've provided, you will find this to be one mystery that is easy to solve. Even when one of your suggestions is not a hit with a reader, don't be discouraged. A 100 percent success rate in readers' advisory just isn't going to happen; there's an unending variety of readers and myriad reading choices. True satisfaction in readers' advisory work comes from knowing that readers are comfortable sharing their love of books with you and that they find your library to be a place where people are always willing to talk with them about mysteries.

NOTE

1. Rosemary Herbert, ed., *The Oxford Companion to Crime and Mystery Writing* (New York: Oxford University Press, 1999), 97.

Checklist for a Successful
Mystery Readers' Advisory Interview

☐ What exactly does the reader mean by "mystery"? Are they talking about authors such as Agatha Christie and Robert Parker, or are they thinking more of suspense writers such as Mary Higgins Clark?

☐ Does the reader want a certain subgenre of mystery?

☐ What elements matter most to the reader? Is it the mood, writing style, setting, type of character, pace of the story, or some combination of all of these?

☐ How much violence, graphic language, and sex is the reader comfortable with in a mystery?

☐ What is it about a mystery that appeals most to the reader: solving a puzzling plot, finding a protagonist to whom he or she can easily relate, or a certain theme?

☐ Is the reader interested in a stand-alone mystery, or does the reader want a series that will keep him or her busy for a while?

☐ What format—print, audio, video—does the reader want?

☐ Is the reader willing to try some nonfiction mystery crossovers?

10

MYSTERY RESOURCES

With more than one thousand mysteries being released each year, in addition to the wealth of classic mystery titles sitting on the shelves of our libraries, most of us find it difficult, if not impossible, to keep up with all the books. On top of this, when suggesting titles to our readers, if we are forced to rely solely on those books we ourselves have read, many of us would run out of choices before our readers came back for seconds. Fortunately, there are resources that can help keep us on the top of the mystery readers' advisory game.

These resources are the secret weapons you can use to stay current with the latest in mystery fiction. Before we talk about these resources, we first need to clarify two important points about readers' advisory work that apply to all fiction genres. First, readers' advisory service is about suggesting books that readers might enjoy. It is not possible to guarantee that a particular book will meet every reader's expectations at any given point in time. There are just too many variables.

Second, being a good readers' advisor does not mean that you have to have personally read, and enjoyed, every title you offer a reader. This is an impossible goal. Being a good readers' advisor simply means knowing enough about a particular title—whether through your own reading or through information you have gathered from other sources—that you can reasonably expect that an individual reader may be interested in it. This is where mystery resources—print, online, and associations—can be of immense help.

BY THE BOOK: PRINT RESOURCES

Unfortunately, there is no one single, all-purpose, multiuse, and suitable-for-every-question mystery readers' advisory reference book. This is why a good mystery readers' advisory reference collection should contain a number of different titles. You can quickly grab and use some reference sources, such as *By a Woman's Hand*, in the midst of a readers' advisory interview, because the information they provide on authors is concise and to the point. Other titles, such as *Mystery and Suspense Writers*, are better suited to a quiet time (well, one can always hope) at the desk when you can read through the book's collection of richly detailed author essays to gain a better understanding of an author's place in the genre.

Most libraries will want to keep a few of the most useful mystery readers' advisory sources handy to the reference desk, because nothing breaks the flow of a readers' advisory interview more than having to search for a reference book you need. However, don't make the mistake that these mystery reference sources are useful only to library staff. Consider purchasing a few of the more reasonably priced guides for your circulating collection for your readers to use themselves.

As you build up your mystery readers' advisory reference collection, it can be quite tempting to discard an old copy of a reference book when a new edition arrives. When it comes to weeding your mystery readers' advisory sources, however, the watchword is *caution.* Some newer editions do not include all of the previous material when they are updated, such as *The St. James Guide to Crime and Mystery Writers*, which with each addition drops a few older authors and adds in a few new authors. Whenever possible, don't get rid of older editions of titles such as these, or you will lose some valuable information.

Listed here are our favorite, must-have mystery readers' advisory resources. Unfortunately, many are currently out of print, but we have still included them on our list because they are the foundation of any good mystery readers' advisory reference collection (and one can always hope that these books will one day be revised and republished). We have starred (with an asterisk) the top three titles that are a must-have for any library, whereas the rest of the books on our list will add useful depth to a truly comprehensive mystery readers' advisory reference collection.

Anderson, Patrick. *The Triumph of the Thriller: How Cops, Crooks, and Cannibals Captured Popular Fiction*. New York: Random House, 2006.

Anderson, thriller reviewer for the *Washington Post*, includes more than just mysteries in his critical analysis of the genre, but he includes all the important names—Conan Doyle, Christie, Hammett, Chandler—in addition to a wealth of contemporary suspense and thriller writers. This strongly opinionated resource will help you understand how easily the line between mystery and suspense fiction can blur.

Dubose, Martha Hailey. *Women of Mystery: The Lives and Works of Notable Women Crime Novelists*. New York: St. Martin's Press, Minotaur, 2000.

From Anna Katharine Green (the "founding mother" of mystery fiction) to Sue Grafton, Dubose offers a thorough and thoughtful critique of these authors and their place in the genre. Dubose does an especially good job with the Golden Age mystery writers.

Haycraft, Howard. *Murder for Pleasure: The Life and Times of the Detective Story*. New York: Appleton-Century, 1941.

Haycraft, who at one point was president of H. W. Wilson Company, wrote one of the first histories of the mystery. His work is particularly strong on late-nineteenth-century and early-twentieth-century writers and is now considered a classic.

Heising, Willetta L. *Detecting Men*. Dearborn, MI: Purple Moon Press, 1998.

_____. *Detecting Women 3*. Dearborn, MI: Purple Moon Press, 1999.

These books contain concise information about author and series, but the real value is in the detailed listing of books in series order and the appendixes listing characters, mysteries by geographic location, and more. Even though they don't include today's hot mystery titles and authors, Heising provides access points to many of the older and sometimes overlooked mystery treasures in your library stacks.

*Herbert, Rosemary. *The Oxford Companion to Crime and Mystery Writing*. New York: Oxford University Press, 1999.

_____. *Whodunit? A Who's Who in Crime and Mystery Writing*. New York: Oxford University Press, 2003.

Need to know the difference between *noir* and *cozy*? Are you getting John D. MacDonald, Philip MacDonald, and Ross Macdonald all mixed up? Herbert's book, with its easy-to-use alphabetic entries on authors, sleuths, books, subgenres, terms, and history, will be a ready reference readers' advisory godsend. With *Whodunit?*, Herbert updates *The Oxford Companion to Crime and Mystery Writing* by adding in some newer authors (and dropping some entries, such as "mystery themes").

Huang, Jim, ed. *100 Favorite Mysteries of the Century, Selected by the Independent Mystery Booksellers Association.* Carmel, IN: Crum Creek Press, 2000.

If you want to understand the enduring appeal of some of the genre's greatest mysteries (and haven't had time to read the books yourself), Huang's resource will help. Mystery booksellers from around the United States select their favorite mystery of all time and then write a short—two- or three-paragraph—essay on why the mystery is a masterpiece.

_____. *They Died in Vain: Overlooked, Underappreciated, and Forgotten Mystery Novels.* Carmel, IN: Crum Creek Press, 2002.

In a series of short essays, booksellers, reviewers, and critics go beyond the best sellers and classic mystery titles to recommend one hundred mystery novels that they believe deserve to be rediscovered. This wonderfully quirky book will help you learn more about mystery writers who don't hit the *New York Times* best-seller list (but are still worth reading).

Huang, Jim, and Austin Luger, eds. *Mystery Muses: 100 Classics That Inspire Today's Mystery Writers.* Carmel, IN: Crum Creek Press, 2006.

If you need a quick review of the mystery genre's greatest hits, this is the resource. The authors asked one hundred contemporary mystery authors to write a short essay on the classic mystery novel that inspired them to become a writer.

King, Nina, with Robin Winks. *Crimes of the Scene: A Mystery Novel Guide for the International Traveler.* New York: St. Martin's Press, 1997.

If you have readers who want a mystery set in the location of their next trip (or just have readers who enjoy armchair travel), this is a terrific resource. Each chapter begins with an essay on a country, followed by a reading list of suggested mystery authors and titles.

Klein, Kathleen Gregory, ed. *Great Women Mystery Writers: Classic to Contemporary.* Westport, CT: Greenwood Press, 1994.

This work includes biocritical essays on 117 of the most important female mystery writers of the nineteenth and twentieth centuries, with details about both their works and their place in the genre. The recommendations of each author's "best" books and suggested read-alike authors are especially valuable.

Miller, Ron. *Mystery! A Celebration: Stalking Public Television's Greatest Sleuths*. San Francisco: KQED Books, 1996.

A comprehensive compendium of the program's most famous shows (at least through the mid-1990s), with information on everything from the hosts—who can forget Vincent Price?—to the actors and the mystery writers whose works inspired the shows themselves. A terrific resource for answering those mystery film readers' advisory questions or for ideas on what to buy for your library's media collection.

Murphy, Bruce F. *The Encyclopedia of Murder and Mystery*. New York: St. Martin's Press, Minotaur, 1999.

A good, ready reference source—alphabetic entries include mystery authors, titles, and so on—but you will need to take Murphy's strong, sometimes crotchety opinions (especially his thoughts on cat detectives) with a grain of salt.

Niebuhr, Gary Warren. *Caught Up in Crime: A Reader's Guide to Crime Fiction and Nonfiction*. Englewood, CO: Libraries Unlimited, 2009.

An insightful guide to crime novels and nonfiction works. Includes information on the history of this genre and basics on collection development. Very useful with the current readers' advisory trend in crossing over from fiction to nonfiction.

*_____. *Make Mine a Mystery: A Reader's Guide to Mystery and Detective Fiction*. Englewood, CO: Libraries Unlimited, 2003.

Part of Libraries Unlimited's Genreflecting series, Niebuhr's guide provides not only chapters dedicated to a selection of both classic and modern sleuths but also helpful tips on mystery readers' advisory work and collection development. Need to know which book came first in a mystery series? Niebuhr provides an annotated list of books by author that will help you steer your patrons to the first Amelia Peabody mystery and tell you which one is which.

_____. *Make Mine a Mystery II: A Reader's Guide to Mystery and Detective Fiction*. Englewood, CO: Libraries Unlimited, 2011.

Niebuhr updates *Make Mine a Mystery* with the addition of new authors and titles. This work includes seven hundred mystery titles arranged by type of sleuth: amateur, public, and private detective.

Pederson, Jay P., and Taryn Benbow-Pfalzgraf, eds. *The St. James Guide to Crime and Mystery Authors*, 4th ed. Detroit: St. James Press, 1996.

One in the St. James Guide to Writers series (formerly known as the Twentieth-Century Writers series) this guide includes short biographies and critical articles discussing English-language authors of crime, mystery, and thriller fiction. Although the quality of the essays can vary from mediocre to really excellent, if you don't know anything about a mystery author, this is a good starting point to get an idea of their place in the genre.

Penzler, Otto. *101 Greatest Films of Mystery and Suspense.* New York: Simon and Schuster, 2000.

Compiled by the knowledgeable Penzler (owner of the famous Mysterious Bookshop in New York), this work includes cast lists, behind-the-scenes gossip, and plot twists. An excellent resource for helping your mystery readers find great movies and for developing a knockout mystery movie collection.

Penzler, Otto, and Mickey Friedman. *The Crown Crime Companion: The 100 Top Mystery Novels of All Time.* New York: Crown, 1995.

Not only does the priceless book contain an annotated listing of the top one hundred mystery novels ever written (chosen by members of the Mystery Writers of America), it also lists members' top ten favorites in different categories such as historical mysteries and private detective novels. Each of the category lists is introduced by a master writer; for example Joseph Wambaugh talks about police procedurals. But wait, there's more: a full list of the Edgar nominees and winners up to the year 1994.

Saricks, Joyce. *The Readers' Advisory Guide to Genre Fiction.* Chicago: American Library Association, 2009.

Organized by appeal factor, Saricks's book devotes a chapter to mystery fiction and talks about key authors and critical components of the genre. Anyone new to mystery readers' advisory work will find this to be a good introduction to the genre.

Stine, Kate, ed. *The Armchair Detective Book of Lists.* New York: Mysterious Press, 1995.

In addition to a comprehensive listing of the Edgar Award winners and finalists up to the mid-1990s, this offers great lists of best mysteries, best detectives, and so on.

*Swanson, Jean, and Dean James. *By A Woman's Hand: A Guide to Mystery Fiction by Women.* New York: Berkley, 1994.

_____. *By a Woman's Hand: A Guide to Mystery Fiction by Women,* 2nd ed. New York: Berkley, 1996.

These volumes feature clear, concise profiles of women mystery writers and their best-known books up to the mid-1990s, including heroines and leading characters, pseudonyms, writing styles, and suggestions for read-alike authors. Do keep both editions, as the authors covered in each edition vary.

Symons, Julian. *Bloody Murder: From the Detective Story to the Crime Novel,* 3rd ed. New York: Mysterious Press, 1992.

An astute—if a bit acerbic—guide to the genre by a noted British mystery critic and author. If you can read only one history of the genre, this is the one to read.

Winks, Robin W., with Maureen Corrigan. *Mystery and Suspense Writers: The Literature of Crime, Detection, and Espionage,* 2 vols. New York: Charles Scribner's Sons, 1998.

Thorough, scholarly essays on the lives and works of more than sixty mystery and suspense writers with more than a dozen essays on different mystery themes, including historical and religious mysteries. Expensive but worth it for serious mystery collections.

Winn, Dilys. *Murder Ink: Revived, Revised, Still Unrepentant,* 2nd ed. New York: Workman, 1984.

Originally published in 1977 and then revised, this was one of the first guides to the genre written for fans and readers. Although this works best as more of a browsing resource, it is not without its own quirky brand of charm and usefulness.

PULP TREASURES: MYSTERY GENRE PERIODICALS

At a time when many libraries are cutting back on their periodicals in favor of online databases, why should you subscribe to magazines dedicated to mystery fiction? The answer is easy: mystery magazines are a truly underrated resource. Although it is easy to find reviews of the top-tier mystery titles in review sources such as *Booklist, Library Journal,* and *Publishers Weekly,* mystery genre publications such as *Deadly Pleasures* and

Mystery Scene Magazine provide broader coverage of all the mysteries—including those increasingly popular paperback original titles—published each year. Want to see some of the best mystery short stories being written before the Edgar committee chooses its finalists? Then you and your patrons need a subscription to *Alfred Hitchcock's Mystery Magazine* and *Ellery Queen's Mystery Magazine.* If your budget is really limited, at least consider adding the starred titles here to your collection. (Note: addresses, subscription information, and URLs were current at time of publication.)

Alfred Hitchcock's Mystery Magazine. ISSN 0002-5224. PO Box 54011, Boulder, CO, 80322-4011. Tel.: 800-333-3311, ext. 4000. $33.97 per year. Published monthly except for a July–August double issue.

Short stories by some of today's top mystery writers. Also includes one or more classic mystery short stories and a mystery book-review column.

Deadly Pleasures. ISSN 1069-6601. PO Box 969, Bountiful, UT, 84011–0969. $14 per year. Published quarterly. www.deadlypleasures.com.

A terrific resource that includes interviews with mystery authors, reviews of current mystery and suspense titles, and articles on collecting mystery fiction. The "Reviewed to Death" column, in which several different critics and readers all review the same mystery title, is just one of the benefits of this periodical.

Ellery Queen's Mystery Magazine. ISSN 0012-6328. PO Box 54052, Boulder, CO, 80322-4052. Tel.: 800-333-3053. $33.97 per year. Published monthly except for a combined September–October issue.

Includes mystery short stories by a wide range of authors and a book review column.

Mystery Scene Magazine. 331 W. 57th Street, Suite 148, New York, NY, 10019. Tel.: 212-765-7124. $32. Published five times a year. www.mysteryscenemag.com.

Established in 1985, *Mystery Scene Magazine* is the "oldest, largest, and most authoritative guide to crime fiction." It features great articles on past and present mystery authors, as well as a considerable number of reviews (including reviews of current mystery films and television series).

Mystery Readers Journal: The Journal of Mystery Readers International. ISSN 1043-3473. Mystery Readers International, PO Box 8116,

Berkeley, CA, 94707. Tel.: 510-845-3600. $24 (includes one-year membership in society). Published quarterly. www.mystery readers.org.

Each issue focuses on a particular theme, such as mysteries set in France, religious mysteries, or gardening mysteries, which makes this invaluable for those times when you have a reader who wants a listing of mysteries by theme. Includes articles about the theme, essays by authors who write that type of mystery, and book reviews.

SPIN A DEADLY WEB: ONLINE MYSTERY RESOURCES

As anyone of us who has been working in a library for the past decade knows, web-based resources have some unique advantages over their print-based counterparts. They not only can be updated more quickly and easily than print resources but also offer a sense of connection and community that books can't easily deliver. So when it comes to working with mystery readers or building a better mystery collection, here are our favorite web resources. Library staff with a limited amount of time (and really, isn't that all of us?) will want to start with the starred web resources.

DorothyL: The Official Website: www.dorothyl.com

Provides all the details you need to subscribe to DorothyL, the oldest and most popular of all mystery listservs. Contributors include mystery readers, critics, and writers who chat about everything from the latest mystery and crime novels to their own writing processes.

The Gumshoe Site: www.nsknet.or.jp/~jkimura/

This site lists award winners, new and forthcoming titles, and author and conference news and information.

The Independent Mystery Booksellers Association: www.mysterybook sellers.com

This homepage for the IMBA offers titles for suggested reading, information about bookseller members, Dilys Award nominees and winners, and more. It's also a good resource for locating mystery bookstores in your geographic area with which you can network for programming. Many of the bookstores also have online newsletters that can help keep you up to date on new titles and authors in the genre.

Mystery Net: www.mystery.net

> Replete with mystery games, puzzles, and crosswords, this site also contains reviews and has an active online group for discussions about the genre.

The Mystery Reader: www.themysteryreader.com

> Offers reviews of books in all the mystery subgenres, and includes a list of links to many popular mystery author's websites.

*The Mysterious Home Page: www.webfic.com/mysthome/mysthom.html

> A generously annotated, one-stop shopping guide to mystery resources on the net. If you need to find out something about a mystery title or an author, this is the place to start.

Noir Novels: www.noirnovels.com

> More hard boiled, you say? More noir? This site is the repository of all things noir. Discussion groups, reviews, and bios of the best in noir mysteries. And there's a gift shop!

Stop You're Killing Me: www.stopyourekillingme.com

> This helpful website allows you to search for mystery books by author, character, story location, and protagonist profession. On this site you can find the perfect mystery book for you, and it lists series in order or by stand-alones.

Tangled Web UK: www.twbooks.co.uk

> A great resource for information on British crime and mystery writers and their books.

*The Thrilling Detective: www.thrillingdetective.com

> If you like your mysteries hard boiled or can't get enough gumshoe fiction, this is the website for you. New short fiction, nonfiction articles, and what's new in the world of PI books will keep you on the computer for hours.

Top Mystery: www.topmystery.com

> If you're looking for info about the classics—books, authors, and movies—this is a helpful site. Fun for browsing, as the index is hard to use.

WORKING YOUR CONTACTS: MYSTERY ASSOCIATIONS

There are a number of different associations and groups dedicated to the mystery genre. Some groups embrace the total mystery experience; others focus on a particular subgenre. Becoming aware of these different genre associations and groups is another excellent way to develop your mystery readers' advisory skills. You will make connections to mystery authors who are part of the organization and might be willing to speak at your library, and many of the associations, such as Sisters in Crime and the Mystery Writers of America, are committed to strengthening their ties to the library community through outreach, grants and funding, and cooperative programming.

Sisters in Crime was founded in 1986 by a small group of female mystery writers, including Sara Paretsky, who were concerned that their books were not receiving the same amount of press attention as those of their male counterparts. From an initial meeting of these women, a national association of authors, booksellers, editors, agents, librarians, critics, and readers was born; the goal was to "combat discrimination against women in the mystery field, educate publishers and the general public as to the inequities in the treatment of female authors, raise awareness of their contributions to the field, and promote the professional advancement of women who write mysteries." Sisters in Crime (or SinC, as it is known) has members and chapters throughout the world. Men are welcome to join SinC if they commit to the organization's goals and purpose. For more information, see the group's website at www.sistersincrime.org.

Mystery Writers of America is a "nonprofit, professional organization of mystery and crime writers in all categories: fiction, including adult novels, short stories, and YA and juvenile fiction, screenplays, staged plays, radio plays and TV; and nonfiction, including fact crime and critical/biographical work." Inspired by the Detection Club, a group of British crime and mystery writers who had been meeting regularly for two decades, MWA was incorporated in 1945, and its founding members include Rex Stout, Ellery Queen, and Erle Stanley Gardner. For more information on MWA, visit www.mysterywriters.org.

Private Eye Writers of America is a group of writers, fans, and publishing professionals devoted to the appreciation and promotion of private eye mysteries. The PWA was founded in 1982, and its members include such notable PI writers as Bill Pronzini, Sue Grafton, and Sara Paretsky.

Known for its publication *Mystery Readers Journal: The Journal of Mystery Readers International*, Mystery Readers International is the "largest mystery/fan organization in the world." Founded by Janet A. Rudolph, membership is open to all readers, fans, critics, editors, publishers, and writers of mysteries. The organization has members in every one of the fifty states and twenty-two foreign countries. For more information on Mystery Readers International, visit www.mysteryreaders.org.

Founded by mystery writer John Creasy in 1953, the Crime Writers' Association is Great Britain's counterpart to the Mystery Writers of America. Representing "writers of crime fiction and nonfiction," the Crime Writers' Association includes many of Great Britain's most famous mystery authors, as well as few American writers. More information about CWA can be found at www.thecwa.co.uk.

WHO IS EDGAR, AND WHY IS SOMEONE GIVING HIM AN AWARD?

Like all other fiction genres, mystery fiction likes to recognize its best and brightest in the form of a number of different awards. Basically, there are two different kinds of awards: fan and professional. Knowing something about these awards and how they are chosen can help you with your mystery readers' advisory work

In addition to awards given out by associations and organizations, library staff will want to keep up the annual "best" lists awarded by review publications such as *Booklist* (which each May does a whole issue dedicated to mystery fiction with its top ten lists), *Library Journal*, and *Publishers Weekly*. Each year a group of members from the American Library Association's Reference and User Services Association (RUSA) nominate their choices for the best books in eight genres, including mystery fiction. In addition to the winning book in each genre, RUSA provides a short list of finalists and some suggested read-alikes for the winning title itself. All the award winners and titles that land on the "best" lists should be required purchases for your library's mystery collection. In addition, they can also serve as a good reading list for staff interested in keeping up with the genre.

The Agatha Awards, named after Agatha Christie, honor traditional mysteries and are given out each year at the Malice Domestic mystery fan convention. The award is a fan-generated one in which convention registrants receive ballots to nominate their favorite choices in different categories, such as Best First Mystery, Best Mystery, and Best Short Story. The

Agatha Awards Committee tallies up the ballots, and the conference registrants then vote on a short list of final nominees (five in each category).

The Anthony Awards are named after the renowned mystery critic and author Anthony Boucher and have been given out at the annual Bouchercon World Mystery Convention (yes, that's named after him, too) since 1985. Anthony Awards are another fan-generated award, for which registrants for Bouchercon nominate and then vote on their favorite titles in different categories.

The British Crime Writers' Association bestows the Dagger Awards. The Diamond Dagger is awarded to a mystery writer in recognition of lifetime achievements in crime writing, a Gold Dagger is given to the best mystery or crime novel of the year, and a Silver Dagger is given to the runner-up. Daggers are also given out in other categories, including the John Creasy Memorial Dagger for the best first mystery of the year and the Ellis Peters Historical Dagger. Only publishers can make submissions for the Dagger Awards, and panels of newspaper and magazine critics or other experts in the field serve as judges.

The Dilys Award, named after mystery bookseller Dilys Winn, has been given out annually since 1992 by members of the Independent Mystery Booksellers Association. The award goes to the new mystery the members "most enjoyed selling" that year.

The Edgar Awards, named after Edgar Allan Poe, were first presented in 1946 by the Mystery Writers of America. Currently, Edgars are awarded in a number of different categories, including Best Mystery and Best First Mystery. In addition, special Edgars are given out, and each year the MWA chooses one writer as its grandmaster of the year for his or her lifelong contribution to the genre. Submission for the Edgars is by publishers only, and a committee of five MWA members judges each category.

The North American branch of the International Association of Crime Writers presents the Hammett Award to a U.S. or Canadian crime writer for a work of literary excellence in the genre. A trio of independent judges selects a winner. The Hammett Award is named in honor of Dashiell Hammett and has been given out since 1996.

The Macavity Awards have been given out since 1987 by the members of Mystery Readers International, who each year nominate their favorite books and then vote on the final list of nominees. The award derives its name from T. S. Eliot's "mystery cat" in his book *Old Possum's Book of Practical Cats*.

The Nero Wolfe Awards are the product of a fan group, the Wolfe Pack, who dedicate themselves to the appreciation and study of classic detective

Nero Wolfe. First given out in 1979, the Nero Wolfe Award is given to one book published that year that best reflects Rex Stout's type of writing.

The Shamus Awards are bestowed annually by the Private Eye Writers of America, whose members select the best PI novel, best PI paperback original, best PI first novel, and best PI short story. The group also gives out the Eye Award for lifetime achievement in PI writing. The Shamus Awards have been given out since 1982 and are named in honor of the lone private eye, or shamus.

Although it might seem that there are as many resources, associations, and awards to keep track of as mysteries themselves, don't feel overwhelmed. Our point here is to demonstrate that you do not need to know everything about mystery fiction to be a good mystery readers' advisor. By efficiently using these resources, you will expand your own base knowledge of the genre and become a more effective guide to the world of mystery fiction.

11

COLLECTION DEVELOPMENT

Effective readers' advisory work does not take place in a vacuum. You can be the best readers' advisor in the world, but if you do not have the books you are suggesting in your library's collection, you might as well lock your doors. For some readers, your library's mystery fiction collection will be their sole experience with readers' advisory service. For whatever reason, these readers will not ask for help at a service desk but will instead choose their recreational reading by browsing through the stacks. If your mystery collection does not have anything waiting to tempt them, they will walk away disappointed and empty handed.

CASING THE JOINT

Many of us think of collection development simply as the selection and acquisition of materials. However, cataloging, processing, and eventually deselecting (or weeding) are just as much a part of effective collection development as picking out books from review journals. But before you can do any of these activities, you first need to know the present state of your mystery collection.

Successful mystery collection development involves a plan and a vision for your library's mystery holdings. The starting point of this process is formally known as collection assessment, but if it is easier, just think of it as getting a bead on your mystery fiction. Collection assessment can be done in a quick and cursory manner (sometimes known as impressionistic collection assessment), or it can take on a more structured and formal approach. Whatever method you choose, collection assessment is the first step in developing a quality mystery section.

Start your assessment process by getting out in the stacks and devote some uninterrupted time to studying the state of your mystery section. Whether you spend hours one particular day or stretch the process out over several days or weeks, it is important to experience the same browsing environment that your readers encounter when they go off in search of a good mystery. Be sure to bring something with you to take notes, and record the authors you have, the condition of the books, the titles you seem to be missing, and which books have an inch-thick frosting of dust.

Comparing your mystery collection against standard core lists is one direction an assessment project can take. In addition to standard readers' advisory reference tools such as *Genreflecting* and *Sequels*, other genre-specific resources, such as *Detecting Men* and *Detecting Women* and *Make Mine Murder*, can be used as checklists to see which authors and titles are missing from your collection. You can also use lists of award winners, such as the Edgars, the Agathas, or the Shamus winners, as tools to evaluate what you have (and don't have) in your collection.

Whenever possible, involve other members of your library's staff in the assessment process. Frequently, your library's circulation staff and pages know more about which authors and titles are in demand than your adult services staff, simply because they see what patrons are checking out and returning on a daily basis. If you have other staff who are mystery readers themselves, ask for their thoughts on the library's mystery collection. One benefit of involving other staff members in your assessment project is that they will become even more aware of your library's mystery collection and may be even more willing in the future to let you know when gaps crop up in the stacks.

Collections are built for individual communities of readers. There is no one standard set of mystery authors and titles that is the perfect match for every public library. Knowing what is popular with readers in your community is as much a part of being a good collection development librarian as it is being an effective readers' advisor. In some communities historical mysteries might fly off the shelves, whereas in other libraries readers cannot get enough hard-boiled PI books. Recognizing these reading patterns will help you build a better mystery collection.

The ratio of mystery fiction to other genres will also vary from library to library. As difficult as it might be to believe, in some libraries, romance fiction or science fiction is more popular than mysteries. That does not mean that a library in this situation can totally ignore its mystery collection. What it does mean is that the library might not dedicate as much of its budget to purchasing mysteries.

The worst collection development trap to fall into is thinking that one particular genre of fiction is not popular with readers in your community. This can lead you to not purchase titles in that genre. Then those readers who might be looking for this type of book will find nothing of interest in your library, which, in turn, reinforces your original opinion that one no one in your community reads this genre. All public libraries should have some books—both classic titles and some current ones, too—from every fiction genre in their collection. It is just the ratio of titles in each genre that will vary from library to library.

Assessing your mystery collection is not an ending point in and of itself. The assessment process should lead to something, whether the decision to beef up your mystery collection or to give the collection a good weeding. With the recent knowledge you have gained about your mystery collection, the postassessment period is also the perfect time to update— or write—your collection development policy. If your library already has a collection development policy, check to see whether it covers fiction. The section of the policy devoted to fiction—including all genres—does not have to be a long, labor-intensive effort. The policy itself should address such issues as the scope of the collection, how often the collection will be weeded, what factors influence purchasing decisions, the number of copies of a particular title that will be purchased to satisfy a request list, and how gifts will be handled.

REVIEWING DOSSIERS

After assessing your mystery collection, you are ready for the fun job of ordering mysteries. Many library systems today might be tempted to completely turn the ordering process over to a vendor to "save" time, but a well-developed and well-used collection is ultimately the result of direct staff input as well. Several factors will influence how you choose mysteries for your library—library type, budget, demand, and collection comprehensiveness. The first factor is the type of library for which you are selecting. Choosing mysteries for a small branch is different from selecting mysteries for the main library in a system. A branch may need only a small assortment of the most popular mystery authors and titles, whereas a main library may need a broader and deeper collection of books that can be shared systemwide. Academic libraries have totally different collection development goals from their public counterparts. Instead of adding popular current mysteries to satisfy the recreational reading needs of their patrons, academic libraries may choose to select classic mysteries to fill curriculum needs.

Your library's materials selection budget is the second factor to consider when ordering mysteries. No matter how many authors and titles you wish to add to your collection, in the end it all comes down to how much money you have to spend. When dividing up your materials budget, it is important to remember to factor in money for ordering replacement copies of older titles; otherwise, you might have copies of Sue Grafton's titles from G through U but be missing A through F.

The current state of your mystery collection is yet another factor influencing the selection and collection development process at your library. If after doing an assessment, you discover that your collection has significant gaps, then you will need to devote resources to bringing your mystery collection back from the grave. Having attractive-looking copies of classic mysteries in your collection can be as important to some readers as having the latest copy of a hot bestseller is to others.

In many libraries, materials selection is done using review journals. Most of the standard library review sources, such as *Booklist*, *Library Journal*, and *Publishers Weekly*, have sections dedicated to mystery fiction and review mysteries on a regular basis. Using these sources is the first step in building a great mystery collection. However, don't rely just on these tried-and-true selection tools. Look at the sources your patrons use when they want to find ideas of what mysteries to read. Many readers are fans of the *New York Times Book Review*'s mystery column, written by Marilyn Stasio, whose wickedly sharp pen manages to convey the strengths and weaknesses of several current mysteries, always in a paragraph or two. Want to know why you have such a long request list for that mystery title? Perhaps it's because your readers saw a review of it in *People* or *Entertainment Weekly*. Local newspapers are frequently the first place your patrons hear about new books, including mysteries, so don't forget to check to see whether your newspaper offers book reviews.

Publisher catalogs are another effective and easy way of keeping up with what is coming out in the mystery genre. Knowing which books are in the works at St. Martin's Press or Random House months ahead of their publication date will help you not only stay on top of ordering but also look good with your mystery readers.

Sometimes, in the rush to purchase the latest hot mystery or true-crime book for our patrons, we forget about the older mysteries in our collection. Whenever materials are lost, damaged, or stolen, they need to be replaced so that other readers can enjoy them. In a large library system, this process can be as time consuming and demanding as the selection of new materials, so it is best to work out some plan for retrospective collection development in advance. One way of handling retrospective collection development if you have a large collection, or if you have a smaller collection but not much time to devote to it, is to break down your collection into manageable pieces. Every year choose to concentrate on authors from a certain part of the alphabet, or pick a few series by popular authors that you can then check for gaps.

The first thing many librarians encounter when selecting mystery fiction for their collections is the prominent role of paperback originals in the genre. Unfortunately, some librarians have some prejudices against paperbacks. Whether it is the misguided notion that paperbacks are too fragile to hold up to sustained circulation or the foolish idea that paperbacks are somehow inferior to hardcover books, these librarians refuse to purchase paperbacks for their collections. Paperback original mystery fiction, however, is a critical component of the genre, and it is time for hardcover snobs to get over these outdated notions.

Many first-time mystery authors debut in paperback. The first several titles in Jerrilyn Farmer's cozy culinary series and Maggie Sefton's crafty knitting mysteries were published as paperbacks. Are you willing to deprive your patrons of reading these mysteries simply because you have a "thing" about the format? In addition, the works of many popular mystery writers are available only in paperback. Need more copies of some Agatha Christie or Dorothy L. Sayers titles for your collection? Good luck finding them in anything but paperback. So the message for mystery selectors is this: focus on the book and not what kind of cover it comes in.

When ordering mysteries for your collection, don't forget small presses. There are a number of excellent small presses and independent publishers that can help you build a great collection. Based in Colorado, Rue Morgue Press was founded by mystery booksellers Tom and Enid Schantz as a way of bringing classic mysteries back into print. Some of the authors they offer include Constance and Gwenyth Little and Stuart Palmer. Poisoned Pen Press, founded in 1996 by Arizona mystery bookseller Barbara Peters and her husband, Robert Rosenwald, offers a range of titles from classic mysteries to new books by authors such as P. F. Chisholm and Kerry Greenwood. Midnight Ink and Felony and Mayhem are two more examples of small presses that offer wonderfully entertaining mysteries for your collection.

WIDENING THE NET OF SUSPECTS

For many libraries, materials selection and collection development does not stop with printed books. Titles in other formats—compact discs, DVDs, and e-books—are an important part of the library's collection and must be selected on a regular basis. Fortunately, the mystery genre is equally at home in these formats as it is on the printed page. And if you don't already have one, adding a mystery media collection can be an excellent way to not only build your circulation statistics but also please your mystery readers.

Libraries that are just starting their mystery media collections have some excellent resources. Reference books such as Otto Penzler's *101 Greatest Films of Mystery and Suspense* provide a plethora of classic and contemporary suggestions that you can check for availability on DVD. Many of PBS's beloved *Mystery!* productions are also available on DVD. Another source of possible ideas is to go through the list of the Mystery Writers of America's Edgar winners for Best Motion Picture (for more ideas about some great mystery movies and television series on DVD, see appendixes B and C).

Audio versions of mysteries can also play an important part of your library's mystery collection. Just as there are some readers who eagerly await the next book in Elizabeth Peters's Amelia Peabody series, there are listeners who wait just as breathlessly for Recorded Books to bring out the same title in audio format. When selecting mystery titles for your audio collection, keep in mind that no one likes to listen to just part of a series any more than they want to read just few books by the same author. If you have Lawrence Block's Bernie Rhodenbarr series or Nevada Barr's Anna Pigeon mysteries in audio, try to get all the titles in the series for your collection.

Expanding your mystery collection to include all different formats will prove a positive experience for both you and your patrons. Not only will your library enjoy the benefits of increased circulation statistics, but also you will receive grateful thanks from your mystery readers themselves, who will be able to experience their favorite genre in an entirely new way.

DEADHEADING YOUR MYSTERY COLLECTION

Very few of us enjoy weeding any part of our library's collection. There is always that underlying fear that we will unwittingly discard come classic of the genre, and our readers will then hate us forever. Well, we're here to say, "Get over it!" It is time to conquer your fears. Weeding is a necessary and critical part of collection development.

Most libraries have only so much room for their mystery collections. Keep adding titles, and eventually you will run out of space. Aside from the overcrowding issue, most mystery collections need a regular pruning to keep them looking fresh to readers.

Like most anything else, weeding goes much more smoothly if you have a plan and some guidelines in place before you just start throwing away books. Decide in advance what criteria you will use to weed a title. Physical condition of a book, circulation history, and number of other copies of the same title in your system are all factors that you should consider when weeding a title. How frequently you weed your mystery collection will depend a great deal on your individual institution. Small public libraries, because of space considerations, may need to devote time every year to weeding out their stacks, but a large academic library may need to evaluate its mystery collection only every five years or so.

Weeding mysteries, as with any other type of fiction, often seems to be a very subjective process. After taking into account the physical condition of an item and its circulation history, staff might feel like they are passing judgment on books with little more to go on than the jacket copy and a vague recollection of how popular the book has been with readers. Luckily, you can also use the same genre reference sources that were so helpful when you did an assessment of your collection for weeding. In addition to standard sources such as *Fiction Catalog*, *Sequels*, and *Genreflecting*, bring some of your mystery reference sources, such as *Detecting Men*, *Detecting Women*, and *By a Woman's Hand* out in the stacks with you to help with authors and titles with which you may not be familiar.

While weeding your mystery collection, give some thought to preservation issues. If you have the ability to send titles to be rebound, take advantage of it. Rebinding books is one of the most cost-effective ways of keeping titles in your collection. Books that need minor repairs should also be pulled during your weeding project and sent for mending. Don't forget to keep track of the authors and titles you are weeding so that you can check for replacement copies.

Mystery collection development can be a daunting task. Keeping up with current releases, trying to replace missing or damaged titles, and weeding your collection can all add up to what seems to be a never-ending job. Fortunately, the time and effort required to build a better mystery collection can yield tremendous dividends. The knowledge you gain of your mystery collection will translate into better readers' advisory service for your patrons, who in turn are rewarded with the promise that there will always be something good and mysterious for them to read at their local library.

12

MERCHANDISING
YOUR MYSTERY COLLECTION

For decades, many libraries have operated under a *Field of Dreams* theory of collection development: if we buy it, they will come. However, when it comes to attracting new readers to your mystery collection and keeping your current readers interested in and checking out materials, this passive approach is not enough. Proactive marketing of your collection is a must.

At its most basic level, marketing—or merchandising, as it is now known—is simply a way of drawing attention to your library's collection and the services, such as readers' advisory, that you might offer your patrons. Although it can be tempting to think of our libraries in a "buy it and they will come" manner, remember that you are competing for your patrons' time with other recreational opportunities. If you do not at least start to think about ways to merchandise your mystery collection and the ways you deliver readers' advisory services, you soon may not have the readers for them.

BOOK LISTS AND BIBLIOGRAPHIES; OR, ALWAYS
ANNOTATE THE ONES YOU LOVE

One of the easiest ways to market your mystery collection is through book lists and bibliographies. With today's stringent economic climate, staffing a public service desk in your library can be challenging. All too frequently, staff who may not be fluent in readers' advisory work find themselves trying to help a reader locate something "good" to read. Having already-prepared, ready-to-hand-out book lists at your desk can save the day. Flustered staff have a list of good-to-go titles that they can suggest to readers, and your patrons can be assured of finding at least one or two possible new reads.

Although it might not occur to us, walking into a library can be an intimidating experience for many people. There are so many possible books from which to choose. How can a person find something—anything—good in the dizzying number of novels? Readers value book lists because they help alleviate the sense of overload that they experience when confronting what seems like an endless array of title choices.

With very few exceptions, any book list you create should be annotated or offer some type of information about the books for the reader. A book list that simply provides a list of authors and titles under a generic heading of "Good Mysteries" isn't worth the paper it is printed on. Readers want to know something about a book before they are willing to invest their time and effort in locating it and reading it.

Of course, most of us work in the real world, and many of us may not have time to lovingly annotate each book in a book list. However, it is almost always possible to provide some information about the book to help the reader decide. For example, you can group similar types of mysteries together, such as historical mysteries, and then provide a few words about the setting, time period, and detective for each title. You can also recycle annotations, saving work you did from one list to reuse on another list. You can also offer quotes (correctly attributed, of course!) from other review sources. Anything readers can use to help them decide whether to try a mystery is helpful.

Most book lists fall into one of two categories: mix or match. In a mixed book list, mysteries from a range of subgenres are brought together, whereas in a matched book list, the titles offered come from one specific subgenre of mysteries. Both have their place in readers' advisory work. With a mixed book list, you offer at least one or two possible choices for a wide range of mystery readers. A mixed book list has a wider potential market even if readers find only a few books they want to try. Although a matched book list will work for a smaller group of readers, it offers them more potential reading choices. The audience is smaller, but the ratio of titles that fit their reading needs is greater.

THE BASICS OF BOOK LISTS

1. Start by determining the kind—mixed or matched—of book list you wish to compile. Also consider where and how your book list will be distributed. This can affect the format you choose.

2. Don't be a book-list tease! When you are gathering titles for your book list, be sure to choose books that your library has at least several copies or more of in the system. There is nothing worse for readers than being presented with a list of titles and then finding out that everything they want is either checked out or not available for immediate reading consumption.

3. Once you have selected the titles for your book list, begin writing the annotations. Other than not revealing key plot points or who dunit, don't be stingy with information on each book. One or two sentences are usually enough to intrigue readers with the title. As you write your annotations, ask yourself these questions: Who is the protagonist? What is the setting? What obstacles must the detective overcome? What is the mood or tone of the story? Is it cozy, humorous, dark, or gritty? Use sharp, memorable adjectives when crafting your annotations, and don't worry too much about achieving grammatical perfection at the expense of readability.

4. There is no magic number of entries for your book lists, but a good rule of thumb is to include between ten and thirty titles. With fewer than ten titles, readers will go through your book list too quickly. Any more than thirty, and some readers start to get that overload feeling of too many choices.

5. Once you have completed a book list, you still are not quite done with it. Every book list should be updated and revised on a regular basis to keep it new and interesting for readers.

6. Although we have talked about printed book lists, don't forget that book lists work equally well on your library's webpage.

DISPLAYS: WHAT ARE YOU LOOKING AT?

The actual layout of your library will play the largest role in determining the type of displays with which you will have success. Some libraries may have built-in display cases or special areas devoted to merchandising their collection. Other libraries may have space to set up tables or exhibits and not affect the flow of traffic. Before you begin thinking about doing any displays of your mystery fiction, take a look around to see what you have to work with.

Libraries generally put together two different types of displays. One kind is meant to showcase a portion of the collection and bring various books and authors to the attention of readers. Think of this kind of display as like a store window, or a look-but-do-not-touch approach. The other kind of display is meant to encourage readers to pick up and check out titles from the display itself. This type of open, interactive display is the kind you frequently see inside bookstores and is the one that we concentrate on.

Once you have taken stock of your library's display possibilities, then comes the creative part: determining the scope of the display. Are you planning on showcasing a particular subgenre of mystery, such as private detective novels, or will you put together a display featuring mysteries with a similar theme, such as animal mysteries? As you develop the scope of your display, be sure your library has enough books on the theme to keep the display going for a while. And here is another tip, whenever possible keep some of your titles in reserve to refresh the display and keep it interesting. There is nothing worse than putting a lot of time and effort into planning a display only to have it run out of materials before the ink is dry on your signs. If your creative well has gone dry, consider the following possibilities.

Culinary Crimes

Pull together mysteries featuring a cooking theme, such as those by Diane Mott Davidson, Joanne Fluke, Virginia Rich, or Katherine Hall Page. Then add in some colorful cookbooks (Katherine Hall Page just published a cookbook with her own recipes, so she can do double duty on this display) and a few clever props, such as a chef's toque, cooking utensils, and an apron, and your display is ready to go.

Murder Makes the World Go Round

Using a large world map as a backdrop for your display, pick mysteries that prominently feature a specific country or city. Put markers in the map indicating which mysteries are set there. For ideas of authors and titles to use, check out *Crimes of the Scene* by Nina King and Robin Winks. Other reference books, such as *Detecting Men* and *Detecting Women*, both by Willetta L. Heising, also have geographic indexes that can help you find titles to use.

Classic Crimes

This can be a wonderful way to introduce your patrons to the classic mystery writers of the late nineteenth and early twentieth centuries. Although the books of Agatha Christie and Raymond Chandler may be old hat to some mystery readers, others have never experienced the rewards of reading these classic masters. Put some biographies of the authors and literary criticism of their works in the display, too. Authors to consider include Ngaio Marsh, Dorothy L. Sayers, Sir Arthur Conan Doyle, John Dickson Carr, Ellery Queen, and Dashiell Hammett.

CROSS-MARKETING YOUR MYSTERY COLLECTION

The current trend for mixing fiction genres—or hyphenated fiction, as it is sometimes called—is definitely here to stay. Although genre-blended books (e.g., fantasy romance, historical adventure) often present some unique challenges (and more than a few headaches to catalogers), these novels also offer readers' advisory staff a unique opportunity: the chance to introduce readers to a genre they may never have considered before.

Try introducing your western fans to the mysteries of Steven Hockensmith, whose book *Holmes on the Range* introduces Montana cowboys and brothers Gustav and Otto Amlingmeyer (also known as Old Red and Big Red). After hearing one of Conan Doyle's Sherlock Holmes stories, Gustav becomes determined to follow in his literary hero's footsteps. Old Red goes on to use his "deducifying" skills to solve a number of mysteries in the four and counting books in the series, all of which have the same colorful literary flavor and unique characters of classic western fiction.

With the dearth of traditional Regency romances being published today, those readers who loved and cherished this subgenre of romance fiction are now sometimes at a loss for new authors. But with the number of historical mysteries set during the Regency currently available, you have the makings of a readers' advisory match made in heaven. Give these romance readers Stephanie Barron's impeccably crafted series featuring Jane Austen (yes, that Jane Austen), which begins with *Jane and the Unpleasantness at Scargrave Manor*. Barron so successfully re-creates the wonderfully cool and ironic voice of the original Jane that Austen fans will be in literary heaven. Barron isn't the only option your readers have. There is also Carrie Bebris, whose books actually take characters from Jane Austen's literary world and give them a murder or two to solve. Several Regency authors made the switch to historical mysteries when the romance market dried up, including Rosemary Stevens, whose books feature Beau Brummel as a sleuth. And Kate Ross gifted the world with four superbly written Regency historicals that are guaranteed to win new fans once you introduce them to your romance readers.

Are your historical fiction readers on an Attila the Hun rampage because Philippa Gregory isn't writing fast enough for them? Send them away with one of Fiona Buckley's masterfully written books featuring Ursula Blanchard, lady-in-waiting to Elizabeth I. Not only does Buckley provide the same richly detailed setting and cast of colorful characters that Gregory gives her readers, but she also skillfully integrates a number of real historical events into her puzzling plots, including her first book *To Shield the Queen*, which looks at who really may have killed Amy Robsart, the wife of Elizabeth's rumored romantic interest Robert Dudley.

When it comes to gentle reads, the last place most of us would think of is the crime-ridden world of mystery fiction, but there are some unique cross-marketing readers' advisory opportunities there, too. Consider Nancy Atherton's wonderfully cozy Aunt Dimity books. *Aunt Dimity's Death*, the first in the long-running series, introduce readers to Lori Shepherd, an American who travels to England to claim a bequest in a will, only to discover that Aunt Dimity, whom she believed to be the imaginary subject of some childhood stories told to her by her mother, is a very real person. The Aunt Dimity mysteries are sweet, charming, and just a bit romantic. The literary equivalent of a warm, comforting cup of hot cocoa, these books would be an excellent suggestion for your gentle-read crowd.

These are just a few examples of the cross-marketing opportunities that exist when you begin to think outside the mystery box and consider what elements in a mystery might work with readers of another genre.

PROGRAMMING: GATHERING THE SUSPECTS TOGETHER

For libraries that have the staff and time, adult programming can be another effective way of marketing your library's mystery collection. The range of programming possibilities is limited only by your library's budget and staff. Programs can be done with limited funds and staff time or with an unlimited budget and plenty of staff involvement. But whether your programming budget is limited to nickels and dimes or extends into the financial stratosphere, the key to successful programs is planning.

MYSTERY BOOK DISCUSSION GROUPS: TALK AMONGST YOURSELVES

The past two decades have seen a renaissance of book discussion groups at libraries, bookstores, and private homes. A book discussion group focusing specifically on mystery fiction can be one of your library's most popular types of programs. As with any book discussion group, you will need to do your homework first. Determine the best possible day and time for your group to meet. For some libraries, a weekday night might be best; other libraries might find that a weekend morning draws more people. If you are completely new to starting book discussion programs, there are a number of excellent general guides, including *The Book Group Book: A Thoughtful Guide to Forming and Enjoying a Stimulating Book Discussion Group*, by Ellen Slezak; *The Reading Group Book: The Complete Guide to Starting and Sustaining a Reading Group, with Annotated Lists of 250 Titles for Provocative Discussion*, by David Laskin and Holly Hughes; and Patrick Sauer's *The Complete Idiot's Guide to Starting a Reading Group*, which includes an entertaining chapter on mystery fiction and book discussion groups. Libraries will also want to consider Gary Warren Niebuhr's *Read 'Em Their Writes: A Handbook for Mystery and Crime Fiction Discussions*, which offers good advice on the ins and outs of starting a mystery book discussion group.

Once you have absorbed the basics of hosting a discussion group, you are ready to start choosing some mystery titles. Because the key word with book discussion groups is *discuss*, it is important to choose titles that will provide lots of lively interaction from those attending. Unfortunately, some mystery books, though highly enjoyable and delightful to read, do not lend themselves well to the book discussion venue. Although mysteries such as those by Lilian Jackson Braun or Diane Mott Davidson are wonderfully entertaining for millions of readers, they may not be quite as successful when it comes to serving as a foundation for serious discussion.

Fortunately, there are lots of great mysteries that do work well for discussion groups. P. D. James's elegantly written mysteries provide the opportunity to both discuss the author's literary approach to the mystery and her multilayered characters, as well as her ability to evoke a strong sense of place in her books. Both Raymond Chandler and Dorothy L. Sayers are known for their stylish writing and thoughtful plotting, and a book discussion group could both find much to consider in their works and discuss how successfully these writers' novels echo a particular time and place. (For more examples of good book discussion mysteries, see our list of choices in appendix A).

Libraries can add a few twists to the regular pattern of a book discussion in several ways. Try tying one of your mystery novel choices to its counterpart on film. For example, you could both read and watch *Farewell, My Lovely*, *The Postman Always Rings Twice*, or *LA Confidential*.

Some mystery book discussion groups might also enjoy hosting an author for one of their meetings. Reading a book by an author and then having the opportunity to get an inside look at how the book was created can be entertaining and enlightening. The downside of having the author present at your discussion is that some members might be reluctant to express their true feelings about a book if they think they will hurt the author's feelings, and some authors might find it difficult to listen as readers tear apart their literary work of art.

AUTHOR PROGRAMS: UP CLOSE AND PERSONAL

Hosting an author program at your library can be one of the most rewarding experiences you have in your career, or it can be a nightmare. Which way it turns out is really up to you. Readers love to hear their favorite authors talk about their work, and many authors love interacting with their readers, but if you want to increase the odds that your program is a success, heed the following advice. (Libraries that do a lot of author programming will also want to invest in a copy of Chapple Langemack's excellent book *The Author Event Planner: How to Plan, Execute, and Enjoy Author Events*.)

The most important ingredient in your author program is the author him- or herself. Choosing the right author for your program requires advance planning, a certain amount of flexibility, and a little bit of luck. First of all, not every author is comfortable speaking to groups. If an author seems reluctant to accept your offer to do a program, respect his or her wishes and don't try to coax the author into doing so. There is nothing worse than watching someone stumble through a talk when both you and your audience know that the speaker would rather be anywhere else than standing in front of them.

However, if an author who wants to do a program for you approaches your library, do a bit of checking before immediately accepting the offer. Ask the author if he or she has done programs for any other groups or libraries in the area. If possible, try to contact those groups and ask how the program went. Your first responsibility to your patrons is to provide the best program you can. It may be necessary at times to gently and politely dissuade an author from doing a program if you do not feel it will work out for your library.

Your library's programming facilities will play a major role in determining which authors you should consider engaging. If you have only a small room that seats twenty-five people, asking Sue Grafton to come and speak would probably be a mistake. Conversely, if the only programming space you have is an auditorium that seats three hundred, asking a relatively new and unknown author to speak there might be less than rewarding. If the program brings in only ten or fifteen people, seeing them scattered through such a cavernous setting might disappoint the author. The key is to match the programming facilities you have to the anticipated audience for an author.

Once you have found an author to speak, both parties need to understand the expectations for the program. First decide on the kind of program you will be offering. It is going to be just a book signing with the author chatting with readers while signing books? Or will the author provide a formal talk? What is the time frame for the program? Who will be responsible for publicizing the program? Does the author have a speaking fee, and does he or she expect to be reimbursed for travel expenses?

If you are planning on combining an author talk with a book signing, determine in advance who is providing the books. If the author is bringing copies of a book, will the author need help selling them? Should you plan on having change handy for those who don't have the exact amount needed to purchase the book? If the library is responsible for providing copies of the books, how will you get them to the program and who is going to sell them? If you have a local bookstore that is willing to team up with you for a program, count your blessings! Letting the bookstore handle the hassles of providing copies and selling books at the program is more than worth letting them keep whatever profits might result from the program.

At least a month before your program, confirm the details with your author. If the author is coming from out of town, ask if he or she needs directions to your library and be prepared to offer instructions for parking. Confirm any last-minute details such as whether the author will need an introduction, if he or she will be bringing guests, and if there are any audiovisual requirements other than a microphone.

On the day of the program, arrive early. Check to see that your seating arrangements are set. If you are serving refreshments, see to it that these preparations are under way. If your author is signing books, have a separate table set up, along with several pens. Once your author has arrived, greet him or her warmly and go over any last-minute instructions. Gently remind the author of the time frame of the program, and let the author know that you'll signal when it is time to wrap things up. If the author plans on taking questions from the audience during the talk, keep this programming trick in mind: have someone (a fellow employee, a friend, or a volunteer) planted in the audience with one or two questions to get the ball rolling. Sometimes it takes one person to break the ice before others feel comfortable asking questions.

Be sure to thank your author after the program, and always follow up with a written thank-you note. Author programs can be a lot of work, but with practice you will find they get easier. And nothing replaces the glow you get from a well-attended program that is a hit with both the speaker and your patrons.

BOOKTALKING: SELL THAT MYSTERY!

At its most basic level, a booktalk is simply a commercial for books. It is a way of tempting readers into picking up a title they might ordinarily pass by. A booktalk is not the same thing as a book review. A booktalk doesn't delve into the critical merits of an individual title or the author's place in literature. Booktalks can be done informally, such as when you are out in the stacks helping a patron find a good mystery, or they can be done in a more structured way, such as through a program. Either way, booktalks are another excellent means of merchandising your mystery collection.

With their exciting plots, interesting characters, and great hooks, mysteries lend themselves quite well to booktalking, and a program featuring a series of mystery booktalks is an excellent way to introduce readers to the literary treasures that await them. Whether as an outreach program or an informal, in-house affair, here are the seven commandments of an excellent booktalk:

1. Don't booktalk any mystery that you have not read. You can't be sincerely engaging about a mystery if you are winging it from an Amazon.com synopsis.

2. Don't give too much away. A booktalk is not a lengthy discussion of the book's plot and characters. It is an introduction to the story or a taste of what awaits the reader. You will not endear yourself to your patrons if you give away key plot elements in your booktalk.

3. Refrain from reading from the mystery itself. Very few of us are talented enough to give the kind of reading that keeps an audience on the edge of their seats.

4. Don't spend too much time on one book. Try to keep the amount of time you spend talking about an individual title to three to five minutes.

5. Include a range of mysteries in your booktalk. By booktalking a variety of mysteries from different subgenres, you are certain to have at least one title for everyone in your audience.

6. Keep track of what you are booktalking. Bring copies of a book list of the authors and titles you are booktalking to the program so that your listeners can find the books later at your library.

7. Above all, enjoy the experience! It can be wonderfully rewarding to share your love of mysteries by talking about them, and you will quickly discover that your efforts are very much appreciated by your patrons.

We've covered just a few examples of ways that you can merchandise your library's mystery collection. Using one or more of these marketing tools or techniques is an easy way to take the mystery out of finding a good mystery for your patrons and to ensure that your dream mystery collection becomes a reality for readers.

APPENDIX A

Mysteries for a Book Discussion

In general, mysteries make wonderful, escapist reading, but not every mystery works well in a book discussion setting. The following titles are books we have used successfully in discussion groups, because in addition to being terrific mysteries, these titles offer that extra something discussion groups need. Whether it is the lyrical writing of *Purple Cane Road* or *Dreaming of the Bones*, the unique characters in *Free Reign* or *Blanche on the Lam*, or the fascinating historical settings of *The Alienist* or *The Information Officer*, we guarantee that these detective stories will give your book groups plenty of things to talk about! (For some of the classic titles on our list, we have chosen a recent edition of the title that is currently in print—the copyright date for those particular titles reflects the current copyright date rather than the original publication date.)

Aubert, Rosemary. *Free Reign*. Bridgehampton, NY: Bridge Works Publishing, 1997.

> Once a distinguished judge, Ellis Portal now lives in a packing crate, but when he stumbles across a severed finger with a signet ring—one of five rings given to Ellis and four of his law school classmates—Ellis has no choice but to investigate.

Bolton, S. J. *Sacrifice*. New York: Minotaur Books, 2008.

> Obstetrician Tora Hamilton has some serious second thoughts about her new home in the Shetland Islands after she finds a young woman's corpse incised with Viking runes on her back.

Burke, James Lee. *Purple Cane Road*. New York: Random House, 2000.

> While working to clear the charges against a woman on death row, homicide investigator Dave Robicheaux searches for the person who murdered his own mother thirty years earlier.

Cain, James M. *Double Indemnity*. New York: Vintage Books, 1989.

> A small-time, small-souled insurance agent plots with a bored housewife to kill her husband in this noir classic.

Carr, Caleb. *The Alienist.* New York: Random House, 1994.

In New York City during the 1890s, a reporter and an alienist (think "psychiatrist") join forces with the police to stop a grisly killer who is targeting transvestite prostitutes.

Crombie, Deborah. *Dreaming of the Bones.* New York: Scribner, 1997.

Cambridge professor Victoria McClellan becomes convinced that the subject of her new biography, poet Lydia Brooke, did not commit suicide but was murdered.

Ellroy, James. *LA Confidential.* New York: Mysterious Press, 1990.

Three cops in 1950s Los Angeles, one sad and flawed, the other two downright crooked, find themselves inextricably entwined in a case.

Hammett, Dashiell. *The Maltese Falcon.* New York: Vintage Books, 1992.

San Francisco PI Sam Spade's partner has just been murdered—can there be a connection with the beautiful dame who begs for Spade's help?

Hart, Erin. *Haunted Ground.* New York: Scribner, 2003.

An Irish archaeologist and an American pathologist begin to think that there may be a link between the recent disappearance of a woman and the centuries-old head they discovered in a peat bog.

James, P. D. *A Taste for Death.* New York: Alfred A. Knopf, 1986.

Scotland Yard's Commander Adam Dalgliesh searches for the killer of both a high-ranking politician and a homeless man, both of whom are found with their throats slashed in London's St. Matthew's Church.

Larsson, Stieg. *The Girl with the Dragon Tattoo.* New York: Alfred A. Knopf, 2008.

To get the proof he needs on a crooked financier, investigative reporter Mikael Blomkvist, along with a teenage computer hacker with a dragon tattoo, agrees to investigate the decades-old disappearance of the niece of the man's business rival.

Liss, David. *A Conspiracy of Paper.* New York: Random House, 2000.

Retired pugilist Benjamin Weaver sets aside his normal work of tracking down thieves in eighteenth-century London to investigate the death of his father, a stockjobber.

Maron, Margaret. *Bootlegger's Daughter*. New York: Mysterious Press, 1992.

While running for district judge, attorney Deborah Knott, the daughter of a retired bootlegger, is asked by Gayle Whitehead to find out who murdered her mom eighteen years earlier.

McCrumb, Sharyn. *If Ever I Return, Pretty Peggy-O*. New York: Scribner, 1990.

Peggy Muryan, a folksinger popular in the 1960s, moves back home to the small Tennessee town where she grew up, but when she receives a threatening postcard, Peggy turns to Sheriff Spencer Arrowood for help.

Mills, Mark. *The Information Officer*. New York: Random House, 2009.

British Information Bureau officer Max Chadwick has his work cut out for him once he discovers proof that a British officer is behind the brutal murders of several local women on Malta.

Neely, Barbara. *Blanche on the Lam*. New York: St. Martin's Press, 1992.

Blanche's past history as a passer of bad checks leads her to take a domestic position in a Southern household filled with conflict—and murder.

Sayers, Dorothy. *Gaudy Night*. New York: HarperCollins, 1993.

A series of grammatically perfect, threatening letters disrupt mystery writer Harriet Vane's reunion with her Oxford classmates.

Tey, Josephine. *The Daughter of Time*. New York: Touchstone Books, 1995.

Stuck recuperating in a hospital bed, Inspector Alan Grant of Scotland Yard becomes fascinated with the case of Richard III, the man accused of murdering his nephews to usurp the throne of England.

Winspear, Jacqueline. *Maisie Dobbs*. New York: Soho Press, 2003.

Maisie's first case as a private investigator seems easy enough—follow a wandering wife—but it quickly becomes complicated as Maisie learns more about the woman.

APPENDIX B

Twenty-Five Mystery Movies

Choosing just twenty-five mystery movies wasn't easy, but here are our choices (in no particular order) of classic mystery films that belong in any library's collection.

1. *The Maltese Falcon* (1941)

   The absolute best in classic noir detective movies, with Humphrey Bogart as Sam Spade searching for that damn bird!

2. *Chinatown* (1974)

   PI Jake Gittes (played to perfection by Jack Nicholson) is hired to check out a straying wife in 1930s LA. A perfect cast, great cinematographer, and brilliant director make this one of the best noir films ever. It's impossible to believe that this film is out of print, but it is due for a rerelease, and we can't not include it!

3. *Double Indemnity* (1944)

   If you know Fred MacMurray only for *My Three Sons* and Barbara Stanwyck only for *The Big Valley*, then this movie will knock your socks off! Bad girl Stanwyck convinces insurance investigator MacMurray to kill her husband.

4. *LA Confidential* (1997)

   Rookie good cop Guy Pierce is surrounded by corruption and sleaze in 1940s LA. With a cast including Kevin Spacey, Russell Crowe, and Kim Basinger in her Oscar-winning performance, this film has become a noir classic.

5. *Laura* (1944)

   Otto Preminger's gritty and elegant classic features Dana Andrews as a police detective who falls in love with Gene Tierney's portrait while investigating her murder.

6. *Murder on the Orient Express* (1974)

   An all-star cast (Albert Finney might have been miscast as Poirot, but the supporting cast is terrific, including Ingrid Bergman, who won an

Oscar for her role) might overshadow the plot, but it stays pretty true to Agatha Christie's book. Currently, the movie is out of print, but we fervently hope for its imminent rerelease. In the meantime, the 2010 BBC production starring David Suchet is an excellent, if a bit darker, choice.

7. *Murder, My Sweet* (1944)

   Dick Powell sheds his pretty-boy image to play (no, embody) Raymond Chandler's Philip Marlowe in the story of Marlowe searching for a client's girlfriend.

8. *The Usual Suspects* (1995)

   The movie has an amazing cast, but we remember only the brilliant Kevin Spacey, in his Oscar-winning role, helping everyone else track down the mysterious crime boss Keyser Söze.

9. *Mystic River* (2003)

   The murder of a petty gangster's daughter reunites three childhood friends (played by Sean Penn, Kevin Bacon, and Tim Robbins) who share a tragic secret from their youth. Academy Awards abound for this Clint Eastwood film.

10. *The Postman Always Rings Twice* (1946)

    Drifter John Garfield plots with femme fatale Lana Turner to kill her husband in this adaptation of noir author James M. Cain's classic tale of greed gone wrong. Lana Turner is so beautiful that she glows.

11. *The Big Easy* (1987)

    This is a controversial inclusion in this list of the best mystery movies, but tears and threats by one of this book's authors won out. New Orleans police detective Dennis Quaid (at his most gorgeous, *cher*) copes with state district attorney Ellen Barkin's investigation of police corruption.

12. *Strangers on a Train* (1951)

    It's difficult not to include every Hitchcock movie ever made, but we restrained ourselves. We had to list the story in which Farley Granger learns not to talk with strangers when Robert Walker proposes a solution to both their respective problems by committing a little murder. You go first.

13. *Gosford Park* (2001)

    Robert Altman creates the perfect setting—a 1930s British country-house party—for this sterling whodunit in which the dialogue is so quick and overlapping that you have to really pay attention to guess the identity of the murderer!

14. *Rear Window* (1954)

Hitchcock again. James Stewart, wheelchair bound with a broken leg, witnesses a murder, or does he? Grace Kelly is luminous as his fiancée.

15. *The Hound of the Baskervilles* (1939)

Many Sherlock Holmes fans think that Basil Rathbone (who in real life spied for the English during World War I) is the only Holmes. Here Rathbone is perfectly cast as the eccentrically brilliant sleuth who travels to the English moors with Dr. Watson to stop a murderous hound.

16. *Memento* (2000)

Memento is a brilliant mind- and time-bending film about a man who has lost his short-term memory and is searching for his wife's murderer. The film begins at the end of the story and goes back and forth in time, so you must pay careful attention. Don't be ashamed if you have to watch it twice!

17. *The Big Sleep* (1946)

PI Sam Spade (played by Humphrey Bogart) is hired by a socialite played by Lauren Bacall. We include this film more for its classic noir atmosphere and Bogart and Bacall's chemistry—the plot has so many twists that it'd be hard for Raymond Chandler himself to keep them all straight!

18. *The Thin Man* (1934)

Mix mystery and screwball comedy and you get this frothy cinematic cocktail (and adaptation of the Dashiell Hammett novel) that introduced the sleuths Nick and Nora Charles (played by William Powell and Myrna Loy), both of whom seem to spend as much time drinking as they do trying to solve the mystery of a missing inventor. Hammett's husband-and-wife sleuth team went onto to star in five other films, but their first case is the best of the bunch.

19. *Girl with the Dragon Tattoo* (2010)

This Swedish film is a great translation of the Stieg Larsson's blockbuster novel about journalist Mikael Blomkvist's investigation into a decades-old murder. The perfect casting of Noomi Rapace as punk computer hacker Lisbeth Salander makes the film especially riveting. The U.S. version is in the works, but it will be hard to top this one.

20. *Witness for the Prosecution* (1957)

Directed by the incomparable Billy Wilder (who also coauthored the screenplay) and starring the legendary Marlene Dietrich, this Academy Award–winning adaptation of the classic Agatha Christie play has an ending so devilishly clever that you will want to rewind the movie and watch it again.

21. *Fletch* (1985)

If you don't like Chevy Chase, just skip past this number. Chase plays an undercover investigative reporter out to bust a drug ring in this adaptation of the Gregory Mcdonald mystery novel. Chase pours on the smart-ass charm and quirkiness, which you'll either love or hate.

22. *This Gun for Hire* (1942)

One of the highlights of this noir classic is the star-making portrayal of Alan Ladd as cold-blooded killer Philip Raven. The second is the oozing chemistry between Ladd and actress Veronica Lake. The plot— does it really matter?

23. *Blade Runner* (1988)

Is it a science-fiction classic of a dystopian world or a neo-noir detective mystery? Harrison Ford plays a detective on the run in the twenty-first century. Author Philip K. Dick was a big fan of Raymond Chandler, and you can tell.

24. *Gone, Baby, Gone* (2007)

Adapted from the Dennis Lehane book, this suspenseful mystery directed by Ben Affleck features private eyes Casey Affleck and Michelle Monaghan, who are pulled into the investigation of a missing child.

25. *Who Framed Roger Rabbit?* (1988)

Animation mixes with live action in this slapstick story of an LA private eye, played by Bob Hoskins, investigating a murder and exonerated prime suspect Roger Rabbit. Set in 1940s Los Angeles, the movie references every big noir movie, from *The Maltese Falcon* to *Chinatown*, and throws in a great femme fatale, Jessica Rabbit, who utters the legendary line, "I'm not bad; I'm just drawn that way."

APPENDIX C

Twenty-Five Mystery Television Series

Whether they are based on classic mysteries or written as original series, television series can play an important role in your library's mystery collection. Here are our choices (in no particular order) of twenty-five mystery shows, from dark and gritty to whimsical and funny, that are bound to keep you and your patrons happily glued to your television screens for hours.

1. *Murder, She Wrote* (1984–1996)

   For many people Angela Lansbury is a legendary, award-winning actress of stage and screen, but to us she will always be television's sweet, practical mystery writer Jessica Fletcher. Yes, it does seem like there is a seemingly endless supply of murderers in the small town of Cabot Cove (which probably explains why Jessica moved to New York City midway through the series), but Lansbury's genuine charm is enough to keep us happily watching this cozy classic.

2. *Miss Marple* (1984–1992)

   There have been Marples before (in particular, a scenery-chewing, delightfully miscast Margaret Rutherford in four 1960s films) and Marples since (Julia McKenzie currently plays the quintessential British spinster sleuth on PBS) but no one before or after has captured the true Marple essence like Joan Hickson (who played the role of housemaid in one of the Rutherford films!).

3. *Poirot* (1989–)

   When David Suchet took on the role of Hercule Poirot for television, he became the most-watched sleuth on PBS's *Mystery!* The series began with the Poirot short stories but soon moved on to the novels (and moved from PBS to A&E and back to PBS). With its excellent production values, superb cast of secondary characters (Hugh Fraser is terrific as Captain Hastings), and brilliant acting by Suchet (who completely immerses himself into the character of Poirot), this series is a must for any library's DVD collection.

4. *Rosemary and Thyme* (2003–2007)

Who knew botany could be so deadly? Laura Thyme (Pam Ferris), a former British policewoman and garden-loving housewife, and Rosemary Boxer (Felicity Kendal), a botany professor who has just lost her teaching post, join up to form a landscaping company but quickly find themselves taking on the roles of amateur sleuths as well. The series offers cleverly plotted, botanical themed murders, and the warm friendship that blossoms between Laura and Rosemary is just as entertaining to watch.

5. *Columbo* (1971–2003)

"Just one more question . . ." Yes, almost everyone knows police detective Columbo's famous punch line, but there is more to this entertaining series than a seemingly clueless detective. Peter Falk's Emmy-winning performance had audiences waiting for murderers' comeuppance, usually just when they think they've gotten away with the crime. Not only does *Columbo* feature some of the most devilishly clever writing ever, but also the television series is an excellent example of the inverted mystery. Viewers know exactly who committed the murder right at the beginning of the show, but the suspense comes in watching Columbo try to prove who did it.

6. *Remington Steele* (1982–1987)

Before he was suave, gorgeous Bond, James Bond, Pierce Brosnan played a suave, gorgeous con man who takes on the role of Steele, Remington Steele, much to the annoyance of LA private detective Stephanie Zimbalist, who invented her boss Steele only as a way of keeping her chauvinist clients happy. *Remington Steele*'s classy, engaging mix of mystery and romance will always remain in fashion with us.

7. *Barnaby Jones* (1973–1980)

Buddy Ebsen was sixty-two when this classic private eye drama (a spin-off from the popular television show *Cannon*) brought Ebsen out of retirement and rejuvenated his career. Barnaby solves his son's murder and continues the business with his now-widowed daughter-in-law, played by Lee Meriwether. Barnaby might be old (and he may order milk instead of whiskey at the bar), but *Barnaby Jones* proves that age and wisdom are useful qualities when it comes to crime solving.

8. *Rockford Files* (1974–1980)

Jim Rockford (whom James Garner plays with an abundance of charm) is an ex-con turned PI who uses his wits rather than his Colt .45 (which he stores in either his cookie jar or his coffee canister) to solve crimes in this classic series. Both the multidimensional characters—including Rockford's father, Rocky; his former cellmate, Angel; and his friend Dennis Becker—and the show's sharp, humorous writing contributed to its success both on the television screen and now on DVD.

9. *Psych* (2006–)

Dulé Hill and James Roday are paired together as a psychic and his reluctant partner in investigations. Roday's psychic abilities are derived more from observation, memory, and luck, but he fools people enough to frequently work as a consultant with California's Santa Barbara Police Department. The mysteries are unique, and the writing crackles with humor, but it is the strong camaraderie between Roday and Hill that really makes the show click.

10. *Pushing Daisies* (2007–2009)

Ned (Lee Pace) is a pie maker with the gift (or curse) of bringing the dead back to life, if only for one minute. Private detective Emerson Cod (Chi McBride) convinces Ned to use his power to bring murder victims back to life briefly to tell Cod how they died so he can solve the crimes and collect the reward money. The witty premise, eye-catching set designs, fairy-tale-like narration, and excellent acting (especially Kristin Chenoweth, who won an Emmy for her role of Olive Snook) make this winning, if short lived, series a must-have.

11. *Kojak* (1973–1978)

Bald, Greek, larger-than-life actor Telly Savalas plays bald, Greek, larger-than-life Theo Kojak, a tough-talking, incorruptible New York police lieutenant with a fondness for lollipops and swift justice. Although the plots were strong and compelling, *Kojak* is especially memorable for Savalas's bravura performance and his trademark: "Who loves ya, baby?"

12. *Quincy, M.E.* (1976–1983)

Before there were *CSI* and *Bones*, there was Quincy, M.E., starring Jack Klugman as a Los Angeles medical examiner. It never fails that a seemingly straightforward police case turns into something that needs the investigative skills of Quincy, even though detective work is not in the M.E.'s job description (as Quincy's irritated police colleagues constantly try to explain to him).

13. *McMillan and Wife* (1971–1977)

San Francisco police commissioner Stewart McMillan (Rock Hudson) and his younger wife, Sally (Susan Saint James), solve crimes as Nick and Nora Charles of the 1970s. Complete with handlebar moustache (him) and bell-bottom pants (her, and occasionally him), they are hip and happening while the plots are as engaging as the leads. A contract dispute with actress Saint James left McMillan a widower in the fifth season, and the series lost some of its charm.

14. *McCloud* (1970–1977)

Dennis Weaver starred as the title character, a New Mexico policeman (based on a real-life sheriff from Taos) transplanted to New York City on a special assignment. The premise is a familiar one (and was inspired by the Clint Eastwood film *Coogan's Bluff*)—country boy among the big-city experts—but Weaver's acting and great writing push this series past the ordinary and into the extraordinarily entertaining.

15. *Magnum, PI* (1980–1988)

Tom Selleck (and his mustache) stars as private eye Thomas Magnum, who lives in the Hawaiian guesthouse of the mysterious (and never seen) Robin Masters. Part security guard, part investigator, Magnum lives an ideal life in paradise, driving his employer's Ferrari, usually with a beautiful, if transitory, companion. Mysteries? Murders? Sure, but who cares as long as Selleck shows those dimples. Sigh!

16. *Ellery Queen* (1975–1976)

This faithful adaptation of Queen's early books may have only lasted one season on air, but what a season! Created by the stellar producing team of Richard Levinson and William Link (who were also responsible for *Columbo* and *Murder, She Wrote*), the show is set in 1940s New York City and stars Jim Hutton as Ellery Queen and David Wayne as his father, Police Inspector Richard Queen. Classically constructed, puzzle-based murders are the order of the day, and the show even has Queen challenging viewers with the statement, "I now know who did it, do you?" right before he presents his solution to a roomful of cranky suspects.

17. *Monk* (2002–2009)

   After his wife is mysteriously murdered, San Francisco police detective Adrian Monk (played with both humor and warmth by Tony Shalhoub) goes over the edge emotionally and mentally and is thrown off the force. Monk then becomes a private detective (and frequent consultant to the police force) whose outstanding success rate is due to his obsessive-compulsive habits (or what Monk calls his attention to order). *Monk* would make a delightfully quirky addition to any library's mystery collection.

18. *Moonlighting* (1985–1989)

   In this groundbreaking series, Cybill Shepherd plays Maddie Hayes, a now-broke, former high-fashion model whose only remaining asset is the Blue Moon Detective Agency, run by David Addison (played by Bruce Willis). Addison convinces Hayes to keep the agency open with him as her new partner, and the two (with the occasional help of Agnes DiPesto—the agency's rhyming receptionist) find themselves solving a number of puzzling cases. The show revived Shepherd's career and made a star out of Willis, but what really makes it a mystery must-have is the sizzling chemistry—reminiscent of Lauren Bacall and Humphrey Bogart—between Shepherd and Willis: the rapid-fire, witty dialogue would fit right into a classic 1930s screwball comedy.

19. *Homicide* (1993–1999)

   Based on the book *Homicide: Life on the Killing Streets* by David Simon (whose book also inspired the HBO series *The Wire*), this realistically gritty procedural follows the homicide investigations of the Baltimore Police Department. The show's ensemble cast includes John Munsch (of *Law and Order* fame), and the show is notable for its efforts to honestly and authentically re-create the difficult and demanding day-to-day working environment of a big-city police department.

20. *Midsomer Murders* (1997–)

   Originally based on the novels by British author Caroline Graham and now on original screenplays, this long-running series features John Nettles playing Detective Chief Inspector Tom Barnaby, who, assisted by detective sergeants Gavin Troy, Dan Scott, and Ben Jones, solves crimes in the fictional English county of Midsomer. Once you get past the unusually high murder rate for such a genteel part of England,

Midsomer Murders turns out to be a devilishly clever update on the quintessential English village murder mystery.

21. *Nero Wolfe* (2001–2002)

Though lasting only two seasons on A&E, this superbly produced series captures the true essence of Stout's eccentrically brilliant sleuth Wolfe (played to perfection by Maury Chaykin), who with the help of his lady-killer assistant, Archie Goodwin (the irresistibly charming Timothy Hutton), always gets his murderer. Served up with vintage flair, traditional murder mysteries don't get any better than this!

22. *Foyle's War* (2002–)

It isn't often that a mystery series is both quietly powerful and edge-of-your-seat suspenseful, but *Foyle's War* manages to be both. Detective Chief Superintendent Christopher Foyle hoped to join the fighting during World War II but instead is assigned to the Hastings Police Department. But the domestic crimes Foyle and his team investigate in Hastings often have a connection to the bigger war picture, as the show's writers deftly incorporate real historical issues, including smuggling, sabotage, looting, and treason into the plots. *Foyle's War* is not only a wonderfully puzzling mystery series but also a moving tribute to the courage and compassion of all those who fought the war on the home front.

23. *Adventures of Sherlock Holmes* (1984–1994)

Jeremy Brett plays (or as some rabid—oops, sorry, "devoted"— Holmes fans insist, *is*) Sherlock in the British television series that became a PBS hit when it crossed the Atlantic. Every one of Doyle's stories and novellas featuring the deerstalker-wearing detective is included in this faithful adaptation of the cases solved by the genre's greatest sleuth.

24. *Inspector Morse* (1987–2000)

Based on the characters created by award-winning mystery author Colin Dexter (who, in the spirit of the great director Alfred Hitchcock, makes a cameo guest appearance in nearly every episode), this stellar series features an odd couple of detectives: Chief Inspector Endeavour Morse (John Thaw) and Sergeant Robbie Lewis (Kevin Whately). Totally opposite in nature, the arrogant, highbrow Morse and the humble, salt-of-the-earth Lewis have different personalities that actually contribute greatly to their success rate in solving puzzling crimes in and around Oxford.

25. *Sherlock* (2010–)

Although some Holmes fans might think that updating Sir Arthur Conan Doyle's classic tales for the twenty-first century is the worst idea since Doyle sent his fictional detective over the falls, we have to disagree. This new series retains all of the classic elements of the original stories and characters but manages to brilliantly translate them into modern times (Holmes has his own webpage, and Dr. Watson blogs about their cases). *Sherlock* is smartly written, sharply acted, and the best thing to happen to Holmes since he matched wits with Irene Adler.

SELECTED BIBLIOGRAPHY

Anderson, Patrick. *The Triumph of the Thriller: How Cops, Crooks, and Cannibals Captured Popular Fiction*. New York: Random House, 2006.

Bailey, Frankie Y. *Out of the Woodpile: Black Characters in Crime and Detective Fiction*. Westport, CT: Greenwood, 1991.

Baker, Robert A., and Michael T. Nietzel. *Private Eyes: 101 Knights—A Survey of American Detective Fiction, 1922–1984*. Bowling Green, OH: Bowling Green State University Popular Press, 1985.

Balcolm, Ted, ed. *Serving Readers*. Fort Atkinson, WI: Highsmith, 1997.

Ball, John, ed. *The Mystery Story*. San Diego: University of California Press, 1976.

Beinhart, Larry. *How to Write a Mystery*. New York: Ballantine, 1996.

Bendel, Stephanie. *Making Crime Pay: A Practical Guide to Mystery Writing*. New York: Prentice-Hall.

Blythem, Hal. *Private Eyes: A Writer's Guide to Private Investigating*. Cincinnati, OH: Writer's Digest Books, 1993.

Broderick, Dorothy M. "How to Write a Fiction Annotation." *VOYA* 15, no. 6 (1993): 333.

Chandler, Raymond. "The Simple Art of Murder." *Atlantic Monthly*, December 1944, 53–59.

Dubose, Martha Hailey. *Women of Mystery: The Lives and Works of Notable Women Crime Novelists*. New York: St. Martin's Press, Minotaur, 2000.

Gorman, Ed, Martin H. Greenberg, Larry Segriff, and Jon L. Breen, eds. *The Fine Art of Murder: The Mystery Reader's Indispensable Companion*. New York: Carroll and Graf, 1993.

Gorman, Ed, Lee Server, and Martin H. Greenberg, eds. *The Big Book of Noir*. New York: Carroll and Graf, 1998.

Grafton, Sue, ed. *Writing Mysteries: A Handbook by the Mystery Writers of America*. Cincinnati, OH: Writer's Digest Books, 1992.

Grape, Jan, Dean James, and Ellen Nehr, eds. *Deadly Women: The Woman Mystery Reader's Indispensable Companion*. New York: Carroll and Graf, 1998.

Haycraft, Howard. *Murder for Pleasure: The Life and Times of the Detective Story*. New York: Appleton-Century, 1941.

Heising, Willetta L. *Detecting Men: A Reader's Guide and Checklist for Mystery Series Written by Men*. Dearborn, MI: Purple Moon Press, 1998.

_____. *Detecting Women: A Reader's Guide and Checklist for Mystery Series Written by Women*, 3rd ed. Dearborn: MI: Purple Moon Press, 2000.

Herbert, Rosemary, ed. *The Oxford Companion to Crime and Mystery Writing*. New York: Oxford University Press, 1999.

_____. *Whodunit? A Who's Who in Crime and Mystery Writing*. New York: Oxford University Press, 2003.

Huang, Jim, ed. *100 Favorite Mysteries of the Century Selected by the Independent Mystery Booksellers Association*. Carmel, IN: Crum Creek Press, 2000.

Huang, Jim, ed. *They Died in Vain: Overlooked, Underappreciated, and Forgotten Mystery Novels*. Carmel, IN: Crum Creek Press, 2002.

Huang, Jim, and Austin Luger, eds. *Mystery Muses: 100 Classics That Inspire Today's Mystery Writers*. Carmel, IN: Crum Creek Press, 2006.

Hubin, Allen J. *Crime Fiction II: A Comprehensive Bibliography, 1749–1990*. New York: Garland, 1994.

Husband, Janet G., and Jonathan F. Husband. *Sequels: An Annotated Guide to Novels in Series*, 3rd ed. Chicago: American Library Association, 1997.

Jacob, Merle. "Weeding the Fiction Collection: Or Should I Dump *Peyton Place*?" *Reference and Users Services Quarterly* 40, no. 3 (2001): 234–39.

Jacobsohn, Rachel W. *The Reading Group Handbook: Everything You Need to Know, from Choosing Members to Leading Discussions.* New York: Hyperion, 1994.

Keating, H. R. F. *Writing Crime Fiction.* New York: St. Martin's Press, 1991.

King, Nina, with Robin Winks. *Crimes of the Scene: A Mystery Novel Guide for the International Traveler.* New York: St. Martin's Press, 1997.

Kinnell, Margaret, ed. *Managing Fiction in Libraries.* London: Library Association Publishing, 1991.

Klein, Kathleen Gregory, ed. *Great Women Mystery Writers: Classic to Contemporary.* Westport, CT: Greenwood, 1994.

Lachman, Marvin. *The American Regional Mystery.* Minneapolis: Crossover, 2000.

Langemack, Chapple. *The Author Event Planner: How to Plan, Execute, and Enjoy Author Events.* Westport, CT: Libraries Unlimited, 2007.

Laskin, David, and Holly Hughes. *The Reading Group Book: The Complete Guide to Starting and Sustaining a Reading Group, with Annotated Lists of 250 Titles for Provocative Discussion.* New York: Plume, 1995.

Miller, Ron. *Mystery! A Celebration: Stalking Public Television's Greatest Sleuths.* San Francisco: KQED Books, 1996.

Moody, Susan, ed. *Hatchards Crime Companion: The Top 100 Crime Novels Selected by the Crime Writer's Association.* London: Hatchards, 1990.

Murphy, Bruce F. *The Encyclopedia of Murder and Mystery.* New York: St. Martin's Press, Minotaur, 1999.

Nichols, Victoria, and Susan Thompson. *Silk Stalkings: More Women Write of Murder.* Lanham, MD: Scarecrow, 1998.

Niebuhr, Gary Warren. *Caught Up in Crime: A Reader's Guide to Crime Fiction and Nonfiction.* Englewood, CO: Libraries Unlimited, 2009.

_____. *Make Mine a Mystery: A Reader's Guide to Mystery and Detective Fiction.* Englewood, CO: Libraries Unlimited, 2003.

_____. *Make Mine a Mystery II: A Reader's Guide to Mystery and Detective Fiction*. Englewood, CO: Libraries Unlimited, 2011.

_____. *Read 'Em Their Writes: A Handbook for Mystery and Crime Fiction Discussion*. Santa Barbara, CA: ABC-CLIO, 2006.

Norville, Barbara. *Writing the Modern Mystery*. Cincinnati, OH: Writer's Digest Books, 1986.

O'Brien, Geoffrey. *Hardboiled America: Lurid Paperbacks and the Masters of Noir*, expanded ed. New York: Da Capo, 1997.

O'Cork, Shannon. *How to Write Mysteries*. Cincinnati, OH: Writer's Digest Books, 1989.

Ousby, Ian. *Guilty Parties: A Mystery Lover's Companion*. New York: Thames and Hudson, 1997.

Panek, Leroy Lad. *An Introduction to the Detective Story*. Bowling Green, OH: Bowling Green State University Popular Press, 1987.

Pearsall, Jay. *Mystery and Crime: The New York Public Library's Book of Answers—Intriguing and Entertaining Questions and Answers about the Who's Who and What's What of Whodunnits*. New York: Simon and Schuster, 1995.

Pederson, Jay P., and Taryn Benbow-Pfalzgraf, eds. *St. James Guide to Crime and Mystery Writers*, 4th ed. Detroit: St. James, 1996.

Penzler, Otto. *101 Greatest Films of Mystery and Suspense*. New York: Simon and Schuster, 2000.

Penzler, Otto, and Mickey Friedman, eds. *The Crown Crime Companion: The Top 100 Mystery Novels of All Time*. New York: Crown.

Pronzini, Bill, and Marcia Muller. *1001 Midnights: The Aficionado's Guide to Mystery and Detective Fiction*. New York: Arbor House, 1986.

Provost, Gary. *How to Write and Sell True Crime*. Cincinnati, OH: Writer's Digest Books, 1991.

Roberts, Gillian. *You Can Write a Mystery*. Cincinnati, OH: Writer's Digest Books, 1999.

Rochman, Hazel. *Tales of Love and Terror: Booktalking the Classics, Old and New*. Chicago: American Library Association, 1987.

Ross, Catherine Sheldrick, and Mary K. Chelton. "Readers' Advisory: Matching Mood and Material." *Library Journal* 126, no. 2 (2001): 52–55.

Rule, Anne. "Why I Write about Murder." *Good Housekeeping*, September 1991, 42–48.

Ryan, Valerie. "Ann Rule: Psychopathic Killers Are Her Specialty in the True-Crime Genre." *Publishers Weekly*, May 3, 1991, 54–55.

Saricks, Joyce G. *Readers' Advisory Service in the Public Library*, 3rd ed. Chicago: American Library Association, 2005.

_____. *The Readers' Advisory Guide to Genre Fiction*. Chicago: American Library Association, 2009.

Sauer, Patrick. *The Complete Idiot's Guide to Starting a Reading Group*. Indianapolis, IN: Alpha Books, 2000.

Senkevitch, Judith J., and James H. Sweetland. "Evaluating Adult Fiction in the Smaller Public Library." *Reference Quarterly* 34, no. 1 (Fall 1994): 78–89.

_____. "Evaluating Public Library Fiction: Can We Define a Core Collection?" *Reference Quarterly* 36, no. 1 (Fall 1996): 103–117.

Slezak, Ellen. *The Book Group Book: A Thoughtful Guide to Forming and Enjoying a Stimulating Book Discussion Group*, 2nd ed. Chicago: Chicago Review Press, 1995.

Slote, Stanley J. *Weeding Library Collections: Library Weeding Methods*, 4th ed. Englewood, CO: Libraries Unlimited, 1997.

Stine, Kate, ed. *The Armchair Detective Book of Lists: A Complete Guide to the Best Mystery, Crime, and Suspense Fiction*, 2nd ed. New York: Otto Penzler Books, 1995.

Swanson, Jean, and Dean James. *By a Woman's Hand: A Guide to Mystery Fiction by Women*, 2nd ed. New York: Berkley, 1996.

_____. *Killer Books: A Reader's Guide to Exploring the Popular World of Mystery and Suspense*. New York: Berkley, 1998.

Symons, Julian. *Bloody Murder: From Detective Story to the Crime Novel*, 3rd ed. New York: Mysterious Press, 1993.

Winks, Robin W., and Maureen Corrigan, eds. *Mystery and Suspense Writers: The Literature of Crime, Suspense and Espionage*. New York: Scribner, 1998.

Winn, Dilys. *Murder Ink: Revived, Revised, Still Unrepentant*. New York: Workman Publishing, 1984.

Woods, Paula L., ed. *Spooks, Spies, and Private Eyes: Black Mystery, Crime, and Suspense Fiction of the Twentieth Century*. New York: Doubleday, 1995.

INDEX

Page numbers in bold indicate an annotation.

You may also be interested in

THE READERS' ADVISORY GUIDE TO HORROR, SECOND EDITION

BECKY SIEGEL SPRATFORD

Vampires, zombies, ghosts, and ghoulies: there are more things going bump in the night than ever. RA expert Spratford updates her advisory to include the latest in monsters and the macabre.

ISBN: 978-0-8389-1112-9
176 pages / 6" × 9"

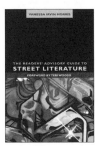

THE READERS' ADVISORY GUIDE TO STREET LITERATURE
VANESSA IRVIN MORRIS
ISBN: 978-0-8389-1110-5

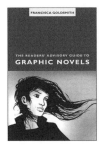

THE READERS' ADVISORY GUIDE TO GRAPHIC NOVELS
FRANCISCA GOLDSMITH
ISBN: 978-0-8389-1008-5

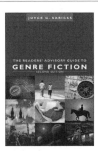

THE READERS' ADVISORY GUIDE TO GENRE FICTION, 2E
JOYCE G. SARICKS
ISBN: 978-0-8389-0989-8

THE READERS' ADVISORY HANDBOOK
EDITED BY JESSICA E. MOYER & KAITE MEDIATORE STOVER
ISBN: 978-0-8389-1042-9

SERVING BOYS THROUGH READERS' ADVISORY
MICHAEL SULLIVAN
ISBN: 978-0-8389-1022-1

FANG-TASTIC FICTION: TWENTY-FIRST CENTURY PARANORMAL READS
PATRICIA O'BRIEN MATHEWS
ISBN: 978-0-8389-1073-3

Order today at **alastore.ala.org** or **866-746-7252!**
ALA Store purchases fund advocacy, awareness, and accreditation programs for library professionals worldwide.